RHO

RHODES

Travel with
Insider Tips

★ AMAZING EXPERIENCES

◎ DISCOVERY TOURS

▭ PULL-OUT MAP

MARCO POLO
TOP HIGHLIGHTS

OLD TOWN ★1
Sensible shoes are recommended for strolling through the beautiful lanes.
📷 *Tip: A photograph of the Old Town from the clock tower is almost as good as an aerial shot.*

➤ p. 42, Rhodes Town

MUSEUM OF ARCHAEOLOGY ★2
Aphrodite, a fabulous garden and a hospital from the age of the knights – all in one location.
📷 *Tip: The many lion sculptures on the garden's terrace provide good photo opportunities.*

➤ p. 42, Rhodes Town

MANDRÁKI HARBOUR ★3
Sailing boats and excursion vessels in one of the most beautiful harbours on the Aegean Sea. Could this have been the location of the Colossus? (photo)
📷 *Tip: Take a photograph of the town from the entrance to the harbour when the lights come on in the evening.*

➤ p. 47, Rhodes Town

PALACE OF THE GRAND MASTER ★4
A palace for the Grand Master of the Knights of St John, and then for the Italian governor – it is now home to the latest archaeological finds.

➤ p. 44, Rhodes Town

NÉA AGORÁ ★5
A market building straight from *The Arabian Nights* serves as a refuge from rain, storms or intense sun.

➤ p. 46, Rhodes Town

ACROPOLIS OF LÍNDOS ⭐8

Head to the tip of the rocky out-crop, with its temple and castle, by donkey or on foot from the picturesque village of Líndos.

📷 *Tip: To take the best pictures at the donkey station, move close to the donkey's head.*

➤ p. 62, Líndos & the South

FILÉRIMOS ⭐6

Some come here to get married, others to watch the aeroplanes landing – but all can enjoy the herb-flavoured liqueur.

➤ p. 55, Rhodes Town

ST MARY'S CHURCH ⭐9

A saint with a dog's head? Admire this curiosity and many more among the religious murals in this village church.

➤ p. 64, Líndos & the South

KALLITHÉA SPRINGS ⭐7

A tiny coastal inlet, surrounded by palm trees, and a lovingly restored spa complex that was originally built for Italian high society.

📷 *Tip: Take your camera into the water to get the best shots.*

➤ p. 56, Rhodes Town

PETALOÚDES ⭐10

In high summer, thousands of butterflies can be found in this magnificent green valley, and even in the local taverna.

➤ p. 88, The Centre

CONTENTS

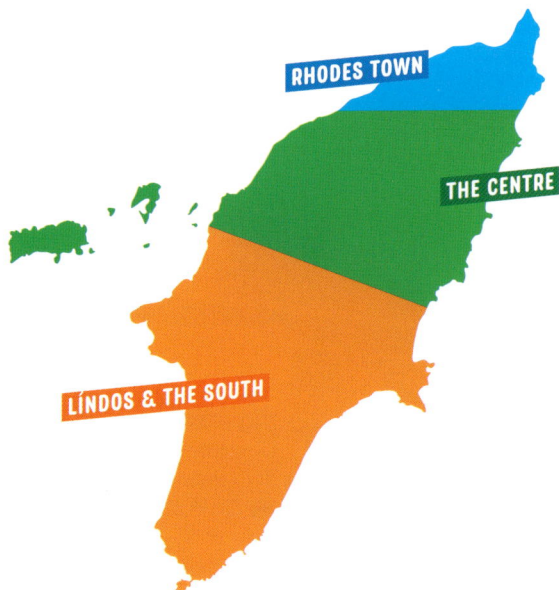

RHODES TOWN

THE CENTRE

LÍNDOS & THE SOUTH

CONTENTS

⏱   Plan your visit

€–€€€   Price categories

🍴   Eating/drinking

👜   Shopping

🍸   Going out

🏖   Top beaches

🌿   Sustainable activities

🐷   Budget activities

👫   Family activities

⚑   Classic experiences

✅   MARCO POLO Bucket List

(📖 A2) Refers to the removable pull-out map
(0) Located off the map

BEST OF
RHODES

Turquoise sea, pink oleander and white houses all compete for your attention in the bay of Líndos

BEST GREEN & FAIR

ECO-FRIENDLY ACTIVITIES

AUTHENTIC & GENUINE

Don't just stick to the big hotels and chain restaurants in the Rhodian resorts; try out small private guesthouses, which are usually nicer, and family taverns, where the food is usually tastier. If you take advantage of what's on offer, you'll not only be helping the local economy, you'll also ensure that your holiday is more authentic and enjoyable.

BIN IT!

In hot weather it's no surprise that millions of plastic bottles of water are sold and then end up in the bin – or, worse, on the beaches. Whether it's a water bottle or a coffee cup, always take your rubbish with you and dispose of it responsibly so that it doesn't become "food" for some unsuspecting bird or sea creature. You could also do your bit by picking up any litter you see at the beach.

STREET WARES

Greek farmers often sell their wares at the roadside (photo). If you stop to buy something at one of these stalls, you can be sure that all the products are local and that you're boosting the income of the producers. What's more, the honey, olive oil, *souma*, wine and fruit will be fresh and unadulterated with chemical additives.

KEEP YOUR COOL

The danger of forest fires in the southern Mediterranean is well known, so take care! Never drop a cigarette on the ground, don't leave glass bottles lying around – they can act as a magnifying glass – and don't include a barbecue as part of your picnic. You should also avoid parking your hot car on flammable terrain, such as dry grass.

BEST 🐷 ON A BUDGET

FOR SMALLER WALLETS

TOUR OF THE MOAT

A stroll through the park-like *moat* that surrounds Rhodes Old Town will give you an idea of the colossal task facing the Ottoman invaders who laid siege to Rhodes in the 16th century. In contrast to the city walls, access is free and possible at all times (photo).

➤ p. 42, Rhodes Town

PICTURE BOOK OF FAITH

The church in *Moní Thári* monastery near Láerma is decorated entirely with biblical frescos, which you can enjoy for a small donation. With a bit of luck, you might even be invited to join the monks for a mocha and a sweet snack.

➤ p. 69, Líndos & the South

A DREAMY SUNSET

If you stay at a guesthouse in *Monólithos*, don't miss the chance to walk up the local hill in the evening (2km, 30 mins) to watch the sunset.

The view of the sun sinking into the sea is hard to beat.

➤ p. 74, Líndos & the South

GREAT PERSPECTIVES – IN EVERY RESPECT

From the *Tsambíka* monastery, high up above the east coast, you can enjoy one of the finest Rhodes panoramas. The monastery's icon of the Virgin Mary is said to have miraculous powers. A look at the guest book will give you a perspective on the motives of those locals who have made the pilgrimage here.

➤ p. 91, The Centre

CONQUERING CASTLES

The strenuous walks to the medieval coastal castles of *Monólithos* and *Kritiní* in the west, and *Archángelos* and *Charáki* in the east are definitely worth it – entrance is free after all.

➤ p. 74 Líndos & the South;
pp. 93, 95 and 98, The Centre

BEST

WITH CHILDREN

FUN FOR YOUNG & OLD

MINIATURE TRAIN

Rhodes has a number of miniature trains called *trenáki*, which run on rubber wheels. Passengers big and small sit in two or three open carriages, and the trains operate on fixed routes.

READY, STEADY, GO!

First, climb aboard the pirate ship, then it's off to the wave pool or the water slides. If you're looking for a change from the beach or the hotel pool, then you could easily spend a fun-filled day at the *Faliráki Water Park*.
➤ p.85, The Centre

FURRY FRIENDS

The island's only animal farm and petting zoo, *Farma of Rhodes*, lies in a completely undeveloped landscape near the Butterfly Valley. Many of the ponies, alpacas, rabbits, sheep and camels can be stroked or petted.
➤ p.89, The Centre

FOR YOUNG GAMERS

Games (including video games) and toys of all kinds and from all around the world have been collected by a Greek and Dutch couple for display in the *Toy Museum*. Visitors can try them out – there's plenty of Lego and Playmobil for kids to play with – and the curators love receiving donated toys for the collection.
➤ p.92, The Centre

PICTURE PERECT

The streets between Mandráki Harbour and Rhodes Old Town are lined with artists offering to sketch your portrait or create an amusing caricature. It might make a good alternative to a holiday snap of the kids, but you'll have to negotiate the price.

BEST

CLASSIC EXPERIENCES

ONLY ON RHODES

A VISIT TO THE SYNAGOGUE

Rounding off the multicultural mosaic that is Rhodes is the *synagogue* in Rhodes Town. Members of the Jewish community, which was re-formed after the Holocaust, give visitors an insight into their history and faith.
➤ p. 46, Rhodes Town

A CLASSIC COFFEEHOUSE

At *Aktaíon*, judges and lawyers get together in the mornings while the cream of Rhodian society gather here in the afternoons. There's also a constant stream of people with time on their hands, both young and old.
➤ p. 49, Rhodes Town

FEASTING AT MAMA SOFIA'S

Things that the islanders love to eat are on the menu in this taverna in Rhodes Town: scary-looking *foúskes* (barnacles) or *simiaká* – tiny shrimps, smaller than the ones you know from home.
➤ p. 50, Rhodes Town

DANCING UNDER THE STARS

Rhodians prefer to spend balmy summer evenings outdoors, and open-air discos are popular. One of the largest is the *Amphitheatre Club* near Líndos, where guests dance under the stars with a magnificent view of the bay and the castle bathed in moonlight.
➤ p. 68, Líndos & the South

PICNIC WITH A VIEW

At the chapel *Ágios Geórgios Kálamos* high above the Aegean Sea, you can enjoy a picnic at tables in the shade of trees with a view across the sea to the neighbouring islands.
➤ p. 74, Líndos & the South

RUSTIC VILLAGE

The mountain village of *Mesanagrós* paints a fine picture of life in the island villages in the pre-tourism days of the 20th century (photo).
➤ p. 77, Líndos & the South

GET TO KNOW RHODES

Hanging out at Plimmíri beach

DISCOVER RHODES

Gigantic walls: the Palace of the Grand Master dominates the Old Town

Your descent by plane starts when you reach the Aegean. From the windows the left, the Turkish coastline and Greek islands appear to blend into o another. Rhodes then appears out of the sea: the island is not a flat atoll, abounds in forests, mountains and beaches. You are about to land in paradi in fact, Parádisi is the name of the village where the airport is located.

INTO TOWN!

If you want to plunge straight into Greek life, your first port of call should be island's capital. The best and cheapest way to travel there is by bus. Depending your bus driver's age and taste, your journey will be accompanied by sounds of Gr rock or traditional folk music. The windscreen is sure to be decorated with fan photos as well as an icon of a saint to protect passengers on their journey.

1000–500 BCE
Founding of Líndos, Kámiros and Ialissós

408 BCE
The three city states found Rhodes Town

290 BCE
The Colossus of Rhodes is built

164 BCE
Rhodes becomes part of the Roman Empire

395 CE
Rhodes becomes part of the Byzantine Empire

1309–1522
Rule of the Knights of St John

1522
Ottoman Sultan Suleiman the Magnificent captures Rhodes

OLD OR NEW TOWN?

On arrival in the capital you have the choice between the ancient and modern, between the city and the sea: on one side are the ramparts and towering fortifications of the Old Town, on the other, shops and boutiques selling the latest fashion labels and umbrellas. There are cafés everywhere, most of which attract a fashionable crowd. Before a shopping trip, take a seat, slow down, soak in the sights and sounds around you. In a café, the waiter will often bring a bottle of water for you to quench your immediate thirst while you wait for your drink. Water is a sign of hospitality and respect to the guest; and "respect" is one of the most important words in the Greek language.

BACK TO THE PAST

Now get ready to take a trip 2,400 years back in time. Leave your high heels back at the hotel, though: most of the streets in the Old Town are covered in cobblestones, polished round and smooth over time by hundreds of thousands of feet. No other city, inhabited mainly by Christians, has more mosques and minarets in one small space, and it's packed with medieval houses too. The city is also home to Byzantine chapels, an Ottoman hammam, a synagogue, a medieval hospital and the remains of ancient walls. Dotted with a plethora of cafés and tavernas, guesthouses and boutique hotels in ancient buildings, music clubs and shops, the city also offers quiet corners for reflection and tiny, narrow streets full of roaming cats.

INSIDER TIP
Avoid high heels

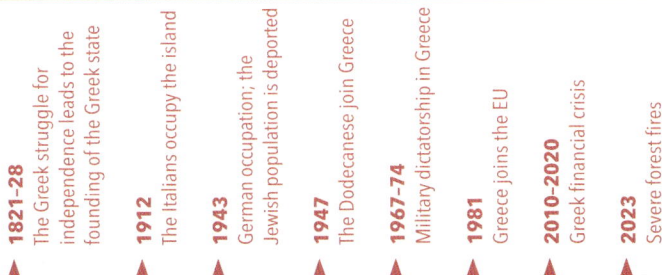

1821-28 The Greek struggle for independence leads to the founding of the Greek state

1912 The Italians occupy the island

1943 German occupation; the Jewish population is deported

1947 The Dodecanese join Greece

1967-74 Military dictatorship in Greece

1981 Greece joins the EU

2010-2020 Greek financial crisis

2023 Severe forest fires

FINALLY, BEACH VIBES

The sea is the city's other highlight. Take a stroll past the yachts, fishing vessels and excursion boats to the beach clubs, where your drink will be served to you as you relax on a sun lounger. You can laze on the beach or swim over to the diving platform. The views stretch out to the Turkish coastline, which is also worth a day's exploration. Maybe you prefer to catch an hour's rest before the evening's entertainment: the city comes alive just before midnight, both in the New Town among tourists and in the Old Town among locals in front of two mosques.

OUT AND ABOUT ON THE ISLAND

But this is only the start of your journey around Rhodes. The island's history will reveal itself when you head out of the capital to explore the surrounding countryside. Ancient temples and an ancient city, knights' castles, churches and monasteries await you – cultural sites embedded in a stunning landscape. The list of sights and attractions seems endless. You can drive through dense forests where giants appear to have played with large slabs of rock. Or why not visit a taverna in Petaloúdes where the chef is sometimes hidden from view by a swarm of butterflies? There is no such thing as boredom on Rhodes.

A BEACH FOR EVERY TASTE

Beaches abound on Rhodes, and they are just as diverse as the island itself. Faliráki has a wide, fine sandy beach which stretches along the coast for kilometres. Snorkelers prefer the rocky cove which once belonged to the Hollywood star Anthony Quinn. Standing on the main beach of Líndos, there are fantastic views on all sides of the wide bay, with the town's ancient acropolis towering above a cascade of whitewashed houses. The beach bar at Gennádi Beach attracts crowds of all-night party-goers who chill out during the day in the hammocks and beach huts. A holiday should always be an expression of freedom, and freedom is highly prized on this island.

OVERCOMING CRISIS

Life is always better when you don't have money worries. The decade following the global financial crisis in 2008 was particularly hard for Greece. The country stood on the verge of bankruptcy and, in order to receive a bail-out from the EU and the World Bank, had to accept the imposition of a series of austerity measures. Salaries and pensions were restricted, taxes were raised, youth unemployment remained stubbornly over 50%. By 2020, the crisis seemed to be over, but then came the Covid-19 pandemic. And when, finally, tourists started to return to Greece, Putin's troops invaded Ukraine and the rich Russian holidaymakers stayed away. Throughout all of these crises, the Rhodians have stayed positive and continued to invest in tourism. Despite a devastating forest fire in 2023, the island recorded its highest-ever visitor numbers in 2024.

AT A GLANCE

125,000
population

Isle of Wight: 140,400

4km
of city walls

18km

distance between Rhodes and the Turkish coast

1,400km²
area

Isle of Skye: 1,656km²

HIGHEST PEAK: ATÁVIROS

1,216m

HIGHEST TEMPERATURE

43.2°C

JULY 2024

LOWEST TEMPERATURE

-4°C

Recorded in Rhodes Town, January 1964

DODECANESE

group of islands to which Rhodes belongs

2,776km

linear distance between London and Rhodes

For a while, Anthony Quinn, famous star of *Zorba the Greek*, owned a home and his own private bay on Rhodes

UNDERSTAND RHODES

BANKS & THE BUILDING BOOM

Before the country was declared bankrupt in 2010, many Greeks were living in a land of milk and honey. Their banks would call regularly encouraging them to take out credit. "What, only 20,000 euros? No, take 50,000 euros instead," the banks would say, knowing full well who owned what land and how much money their clients earned. New building developments were then proposed, making people believe they had sufficient financial means to invest. Many people unfortunately succumbed to temptation: there are still luxury cars on the road and many unfinished building projects.

The banks' generosity stopped as soon as the crisis hit, leaving many Greeks in serious debt. The only compensation is that the banks now cannot find buyers for houses they want to auction, with the only chance of profit coming from luxury properties going for prices above one million euros. However, there is one cause for hope on the horizon: Turkish people are increasingly looking to buy property on Rhodes.

BEACHES FOR EVERYONE

All of Rhodes' beaches are open to the public free of charge – although they can be state-leased for private purposes. Not all of the beaches are packed with sun loungers and parasols, and you are welcome to spread your towel out anywhere. Beach tavernas and bars line the promenades and water-sports facilities can be found in all major resorts between mid-May and mid-October. Lifeguards are a rare sight on beaches due to the lack of funding from the local councils.

BYZANTINE

You will encounter the word "Byzantine" on thousands of brown signs dotted all over Rhodes. The Byzantine era was a continuation of the Roman Empire in the East from around 330 to 1453, a similar period as our Middle Ages. Until 1309, Rhodes belonged to the Byzantine Empire. This Empire spread across all of Asia Minor, the Balkans and Greece. Its capital city was Constantinople, which was renamed as Istanbul when it fell to the Ottoman Turks in 1453. However, the Ecumenical Patriarch of the Eastern Orthodox Church (the equivalent of the Catholic Pope) still resides in the city. The official flag of the Greek Orthodox Church shows a black Byzantine double-headed eagle on a yellow background; it can be seen flying in front of many churches and monasteries on Rhodes.

COLOSSAL

What a colossal man! One of the Seven Wonders of the World, cast in bronze between 294 and 282 BCE and 33m high, the Colossus of Rhodes was once believed to have stood either astride the harbour entrance or on the

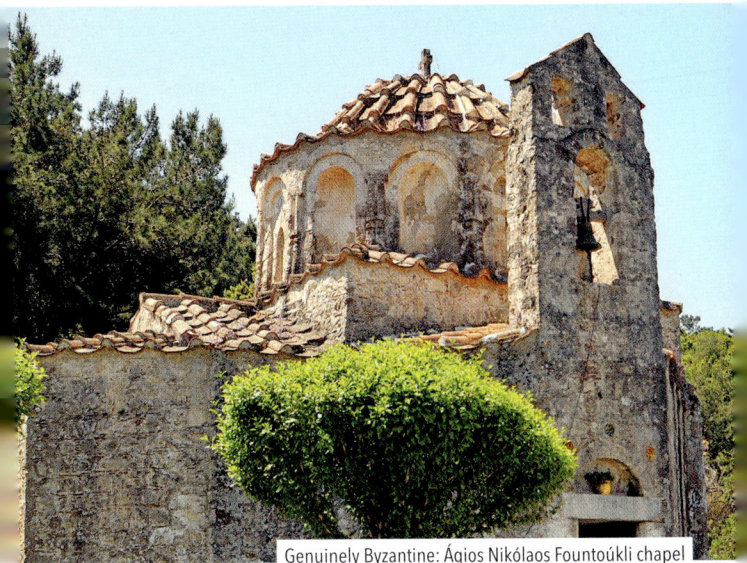

Genuinely Byzantine: Ágios Nikólaos Fountoúkli chapel

acropolis high above the town. However, it has recently been proved that he was located at the harbour fortress of Ágios Nikólaos. Only 50 years after it was built, the statue was destroyed by an earthquake. The bronze was melted down and not a single piece was preserved. However, the Colossus of Rhodes is present everywhere on the island today, with souvenirs ranging from metal statues to prop up your bookshelves to colourful postcards and sunbathing towels.

DONKEYS, CATS & CHICKENS

The Greek relationship with animals is transactional, based on the animal's usefulness. They are not indulged as pets. Cats are feral and feed on scraps, roaming around restaurant tables until a tourist complains. Dogs are there to guard property; chickens are completely free-range, and donkeys continue to be beasts of burden. The animals don't look as well fed or groomed as they might in the UK, but that's because they are expected to fend for themselves or to work. An interesting exception are the donkeys at *Donkey Cruise* (see p. 71) who are too old to work but who earn their keep by going on walks with tourists.

EARLY EU

Around 700 years ago, something like the EU already existed – and its capital was not Brussels, but Rhodes. In the state of the Order of the Knights of St John, Christians from many European countries lived together peacefully and voted in their ruler for a lifetime. It did not matter much where you were born, and land was divided into administrative divisions known as "langues", roughly the equivalent of "languages".

FALSE FRIEND

Nee in Greek is a false friend for speakers of many European languages. Greeks say *nee* when they get married, for example, and it simply means "yes". The commonly used word *entáxi* is another cause for confusion. No, the Greeks don't want to travel by taxi all the time, they are simply saying "okay".

FAMILY FIRST

Do you know all of your second cousins? Young Greeks can usually recite the names of even distant relatives, with no gaps or pauses for breath, and are in regular touch with them by phone. Second cousins are considered part of the family and are always invited to baptisms and weddings. Nearly every bride is given an apartment or a house when she gets married. The bridegroom is expected to have good prospects, but since there is no guarantee of work in the contemporary Greek economy, parents and grandparents often continue to provide support, by using their hard-won savings and sparse pensions to buy a small business for their son or daughter.

GREEN – THE COLOUR OF HOPE

Although the Greeks recognise the importance of protecting the environment, the country simply does not have the resources. With no incineration plant and thankfully no nuclear power plant, the island relies on two normal power stations, an old one

Irony of fate: sun god Helios, the Colossus of Rhodes, was eventually melted down

near Soróni and a new one near Prassoníssi, both of which burn crude oil. Alternative forms of energy have had mixed success. When a solar park developer went bankrupt, many private investors on Rhodes lost a lot of money and locals are now understandably sceptical about investing in solar parks. Wind energy is not exploited enough. The only sector where Rhodes has gained ground is in its use of individual solar panels. They can be seen on many hotel roofs and private residences, and show that the average citizen can make very good savings by going green.

HARPOONS

Kamáki translates literally as harpoon, but its meaning is a Casanova, and it is practically a profession in Rhodes. Adorned with gold chains and big rings, young men and older playboys try to court and conquer female tourists. They see themselves as irresistible and are organised in groups in private clubs. The *kamáki* men are unique to Rhodes, and the documentary film *Colossi of Love* reported on this phenomena. They keep a list of their successes: who managed to court the most women and the most nationalities? They are not troublesome though, and will leave anyone alone who is obviously not interested in their "services". The womanisers see themselves as athletes and stick to "fair play" rules.

IN BEST COMPANY

People on Rhodes do not like spending time on their own. A cosy twosome is reserved for a certain hour of the day.

TRUE OR FALSE?

ALL GREEKS DANCE THE SYRTÁKI

It was Hollywood star Anthony Quinn who made the syrtáki famous around the world. Since he danced it in *Zorba the Greek*, foreigners have considered it the quintessential Greek dance. In fact, the dance was invented specifically for the film, probably because real Greek folk dances would have been a little too complicated for the US audience. In recognition of putting Greece back on the map, Anthony Quinn was presented with his own piece of land by the military rulers of the country at the time: "Anthony Quinn Bay" south of Faliráki. And in the areas where foreign holidaymakers flock, the simple dance remains tremendously popular. During the "get up and dance" stage of "Greek nights" in local restaurants, the syrtáki can be counted on to deliver a packed dance floor.

WE HELPED THE GREEK ECONOMY

The international efforts to save Greece from bankruptcy may have cost billions, but few Greeks felt rescued by foreign governments. People argue that the money didn't stay in Greece, but instead handed on to foreign banks to repay the country's debt.

Otherwise, Greeks prefer a *paréa*: a group of friends or acquaintances who regularly meet up to drink coffee or eat, go to the disco and holiday together. The question asked by friends afterwards is not what the hotel or food was like, but how the *paréa* was.

In case you do have to go it alone, you will always be accompanied by the island's saints. They are present as icons wherever you go – whether in the taxi, in the ticket booth or in the open fields – either as printed images or painted on church and chapel walls and hanging on the sides of the road. You know you are always in safe hands and in good company.

KOMBOLOIA

The *Komboloi* is a set of worry beads, often carried by old men and available in souvenir shops. Although it resembles a Catholic rosary, it is a variation of Turkish prayer beads. The Greeks adopted their own style of bead for relaxation, enjoyment and generally passing the time. The *kómbos*, or knot used to hold the beads together, is regarded as a lucky charm. Apparently it also helps people to quit smoking.

LAND OF CONFUSION

People from Rhodes hate strict rules, and are quite liberal where their spelling is concerned; a custom which can confuse many a tourist. In Greek, place names can be written differently on signs and maps, while the Latin spelling is even more haphazard. *Agía* meaning "saint" is a good example. It is sometimes written as *Agía* (as in the Marco Polo guides) or *Aghía* or even *Ayía*. All three spellings are accepted and combined as the Greeks please. Where there are no rules, there are fewer mistakes.

NO HURRY

Do you know what tomorrow will bring? The Rhodians certainly don't know and don't waste their time planning for the long term. Large events and festivals are only made public a few days in advance, while timetables or the opening times of museums or excavation sites are posted online at short notice.

Vague arrangements to meet the following morning, afternoon, evening or even next week are made, adding the all-important *"ta léme"* – "we'll talk again later." You can then expect a call shortly before to confirm the exact time – everyone has a mobile phone here.

Enjoy a drink and some shade at Elli Beach

TÁVLI

Two men sit at a table with a board, two dice and chunky plastic tokens between them, their heads bowed, muscles taut – do not disturb! *Távli* is much more than just the Greek version of backgammon. It's as much a part of the life of the traditionally minded Greek male, and many a young Greek woman, as the car keys and the mobile phone on the table. You can rent the board game in almost every café and many bars. Just Google the rules!

TECHNO VERSUS ENTECHNO

Beware of confusing the words because there is a world of difference between techno and *entechno* music, although both genres are loved by young Rhodians. *Entechno* could be translated as a "synthetic song": it describes rock ballads with Greek lyrics, mostly performed by a solo singer and accompanied by only a guitar. This music is also appreciated by people who don't like techno. At the current time, Giórgos Daláras *(dalaras.gr)* and Giánnis Haroúlis *(haroulis.eu)* are the most prominent *entechno* artists.

VISITS FROM THE NEIGHBOURS

For a long time, fellow NATO member Turkey was the arch-enemy of many Greeks. Although ties improved considerably in the 1990s, the relationship has gradually deteriorated since the refugee crisis and Erdogan's threat to Turkish democracy.

This situation does not change the fact that day trippers from Turkey have been a blessing in disguise for bar and restaurant owners on Rhodes. The Turkish like to dine in style and, unlike many other tourists, order far more than just a Greek salad. They also appreciate traditional Greek music and enjoy live performances, as the Eastern-influenced sounds are familiar to them. Some even employ the services of an interpreter to translate the lyrics.

EATING SHOPPING SPORT

Al fresco dining on the terraces of Líndos

EATING & DRINKING

RETURNING TO THEIR ROOTS

Mediterranean cuisine, along French and Italian lines, is en vogue, while restaurants serving Indian, Japanese and Mexican food are offering fierce competition, especially in the island's capital. Young Greek chefs and restaurant and bar owners are holding their own by returning to the best traditional style of cooking from their grandmothers' day and giving it a creative make-over, using largely fresh, regional produce.

THE PARÉA IS WHAT MATTERS

Greeks love to have a great variety of different dishes on the table at one time. They seldom go out alone or just as a couple for dinner in the evening, though, as eating in company is preferable. The company of friends and relatives at the table, collectively known as the *paréa*, is considered to be just as important as the culinary experience. The diners always order plenty of dishes, which are placed in the centre of the table. Each person takes as much as they like of whatever they fancy. Usually there will be meat and fish served up on large platters, and everyone helps themselves. Traditionally, more food is ordered than can possibly be eaten: to eat everything is not "the done thing", as it would be a sign of obviously having ordered too little. All plates, even the empty ones, remain on the table. The waiter does not clear them away, so that everyone can see how well the *paréa* has dined.

A LITTLE BIT OF EVERYTHING, PLEASE

You can best enjoy the whole spectrum of Greek cooking if, like the locals themselves, you order a variety of starters – *mesédes* – rather than choosing a traditional menu as you

Kali orexi (enjoy your meal)! Greek starters (left) and grilled seafood (right)

would elsewhere in Europe. You can often even do without a main course. These *mesédes* include various purées and dips which the Greeks designate as salads. Other favourites are croquettes made of different vegetables, also from squid, puréed fish roe and potato *(taramá)*, or your common or garden chicken. The potato patties or mashed chickpeas rolled into balls are delicious. The turnovers, or *píttes*, made of puff pastry and filled with cheese and/or spinach, sausage or meat, are a traditional favourite. Fried slices of aubergine or courgettes also count as *mesédes*, as do fresh salads, pickled fish, anchovies, olives, oven-baked cheese and seafood.

LOTS OF FISH & MEAT

When it comes to main courses, Greek chefs are less imaginative. If their compatriots go out to eat they want meat and fish from the charcoal grill.

Accompanying sauces are rare – at best there will be a mixture of good olive oil and lemon to go with the fish. Jacket potatoes or potatoes roasted in the oven are becoming more popular, but the usual side dishes are more or less poor cousins to standard chips. Dishes cooked in the oven are a traditional highlight in Greek cuisine. Everyone has heard of the famous casseroles topped with béchamel sauce, such as *mousakás* (aubergines and mincemeat) or *pastitzio* (macaroni and mincemeat). Baked aubergines, lamb baked in the oven with potatoes *(kleftikó)* or lamb baked in foil with vegetables *(exochikó)* are all delicious.

FOR THOSE WITH A SWEET TOOTH

Rhodian desserts have a touch of the East about them. You'll rarely find them on the menu at a restaurant; you have to go instead to a *zacharoplastío*,

An old master in the traditional art of making *kataífi*

the Greek equivalent of a cake or pastry shop. There are plenty of these, but outside Rhodes Town they seldom offer somewhere to sit down. Local residents usually take their cakes home with them. The best place to indulge your sweet tooth is to trawl around the pastry shops on the harbour side of the Néa Agorá market in Rhodes Town. The often colourful creamy cakes and gateaux are a delight to look at; however, the apple cakes *(milópitta)* and walnut cakes *(karidópitta)* are considered as more typically Greek. Both can be enjoyed with ice cream, which also goes well with the Eastern-style pastries, such as *baklavás* and *kataífi*, eaten with a knife and dessert fork. Traditionally from northern Greece, *bougátsa* is a turnover made of strudel dough and filled with vanilla custard.

INSIDER TIP
Sweets heaven

HOT FOOD AROUND THE CLOCK

In the more traditional villages and in the towns, most tavernas are open from 9am until midnight. The Greeks eat wherever and whenever they fancy, and not when the landlord decides. Lunch is often eaten as late as 2 or 3pm, and it is common to get together with your *paréa* – your friends or relatives – at 10 or 11pm.

FROM CAFFEINE TO TANNIN

The island's favourite hot beverage is coffee in its many different variations. Whether you choose traditional mocha *(kafés ellinikós)*, instant or filter coffee, espresso or cappuccino, served hot or cold, you must say how sweet you want it because the ground coffee is mixed with sugar and then brewed. You also need to order the milk separately for espresso, instant and filter coffee.

Whisky is the Greeks' favourite spirit, while traditional ouzo, made of aniseed, is also widespread. In rural areas, people like to drink *soúma*, distilled from the remains of grapes after pressing and similar to an Italian grappa. To accompany your meal, you are served water, wine or beer, which is often available on draught. Wines from the island's major wineries Cair and Emery are available everywhere. Lovers of rarer labels should ask for something from the Rhodian winery Triantáfyllou or from Ktíma Papaioánnou and Ktíma Mércouri on the Peloponnese.

Today's Specials

Starters

CHORIÁTIKI SALÁTA
A mixed Greek salad with feta cheese

CHTAPÓDI KSIDÁTO
Octopus pickled in vinegar and onions

PATSÁRIA
Beetroot, mostly cooked with the leaves, but not pickled

Meat & fish

JEMISTÉS
Peppers and tomatoes filled with rice and minced meat

JUVÉTSI
Pasta that looks like grains of rice, baked in a clay dish with beef or lamb

STIFÁDO
Beef or rabbit stew in a tomato and cinnamon sauce with onions

KSIFÍA
Grilled boneless swordfish steak

Vegetarian

BRIÁM
Ratatouille with lots of aubergines and olive oil

DOLMÁDES
Stuffed vine leaves, mostly served hot in an egg and lemon sauce

FÁVA
Puréed yellow peas with onions and olive oil

REVITHÓKEFTÉDES
A purée of chickpeas shaped into patties or balls and fried

Desserts

BAKLAVÁ
A filo pastry filled with chopped nuts or almonds, also served with ice cream

HALVÁ
Confectionery made of toasted semolina with sugar syrup

RISÓGALO
A thin rice pudding with a touch of cinnamon

SHOPPING

Rhodes is a good destination for bargain shopping. You can find a new summer outfit and fashionable accessories, or culinary specialities and the usual kitsch for your relatives back home. The best places to shop are in Rhodes Town and Líndos.

A COLOSSUS TO TAKE HOME

Although nobody knows what the ancient Colossus of Rhodes looked like, you will come across representations of it in souvenir shops everywhere on the island – on bathing towels, postcards, shopping bags and coasters. Of course, it is also a popular image on umbrellas (see opposite).

CERAMICS

Rhodes is an island of potters. You'll find a large number of potters' studios and showrooms on the road between Faliráki and Líndos, particularly around Archángelos. The colourful enamelled wall plates are typical of Rhodes.

CULINARY TREATS

Rhodian wine, liqueurs and Rhodian ouzo may still be transported home in your flight baggage. Pickled olives, herbs, pistachios, coffee or honey will conjure up the tastes and smells of the sunny island on your dining table.

FASHION

You can buy Versace anywhere in the world – but the fashionable creations of Greek designers are sold almost exclusively in Greece, for example in Rhodes and Líndos.

LEATHER GOODS

As animal fur has become taboo in most cultures, the island's furriers have had to adapt accordingly. Many have converted to selling leather, although they often just import items

You'll find everything from olive oil to a new pair of sandals in Rhodes Town

from the more renowned leather-producing countries of Turkey and Italy. There is only one small workshop in the Old Town which makes its own sandals, handbags and belts.

NATURAL SPONGES

Traditional ships operate as stores for sea-sourced items from all over the world at the harbour in Emborikó Limáni, with cheap sponges usually coming from the Caribbean. Natural sponges from the nearby Greek island of Kálimnos are more expensive.

SHOES

Women on Rhodes are an adventurous kind. They like their shoes to have bright colours and unusual shapes, and with heels that are murderously high. Some of these innovations may become fashionable elsewhere a couple of years later, but the majority are only worn on Rhodes. You can also find all kinds of sneakers, trainers and sandals. Most of the shoe shops are located in the New Town.

SOUVENIRS FROM TURKEY

Day-trippers to Turkey should be aware of the customs regulations when returning to Rhodes. The following limits apply: 40 cigarettes or 50g of tobacco, 1litre of spirits (over 22% abv) or 2 litres (under 22% abv), plus items for personal use to the value of 430 euros.

UMBRELLAS

Despite the sunshine, Rhodes is a world capital when it comes to umbrellas. Virtually no tourist leaves Rhodes without buying one. You can find all types, from a three-euro umbrella to designer pieces. Most stores are situated around the *Platía Kyprou* (see p. 53) in the New Town.

INSIDER TIP
Be prepared

31

SPORT & ACTIVITIES

Looking for the ultimate holiday experience? Try horseback-riding through the Rhodian "prairie". More suited to water? Rhodes is not just a sunny island; it's windy too, offering perfect conditions for both windsurfers and kitesurfers. The waters around the island are not only home to fish but shipwrecks as well, making them ideal for divers to explore. Mountain bikers and hikers will find routes through the unspoilt interior of the island. And some of the island's rocks are suitable for rock climbing.

ACTIVITY HOLIDAYS

If you love a rush of adrenalin and exciting thrills, contact *Rhodes Adventures (tel. 69 74 73 14 50 | rhodes adventures.com)* who will help you organise a tour to suit your tastes; it is run by a team of ten who have been organising the wildest activities for 15 years. They can help you book tours and even organise transfers to and from the locations. The activities available include riding and diving, hiking and cycling, rock climbing and windsurfing (both also in conjunction with yoga), stand-up paddleboarding, paintballing and paramotor flights. It's definitely worth checking out their website.

CLIMBING

Rhodes is home to a small group of enthusiastic rock climbers who have created routes in various regions of the island: near Ladikó, Archángelos, Charáki, Líndos and Siána. If you want to try this sport, it is best to contact local climbers on Facebook *(climbing inrhodes)* or take a look at the website *rodosclimb.gr.*

DIVING

Scuba diving is permitted on Rhodes at several marked stretches along the

Wind? Check! Waves? Check! The island is a kite- and windsurfer's paradise

coast when accompanied by a licensed instructor. The dive centre run by young Greeks, *Lepia Dive Center (tel. 69 37 41 79 70 | lepiadive.com)* in Péfki also accommodates disabled divers; the dives take place between Líndos and the southern tip of the island.

Several boats leave daily for dive tours from Mandráki Harbour in Rhodes Town.

INSIDER TIP
Immerse yourself!

Even completely novice divers can take their first dip – down to a depth of 5–6m. Local providers include *Waterhoppers (Odós Kritiká 45, Rhodes Old Town | tel. 69 40 59 84 66 | waterhoppers.com)*, which also has dive stations in Kallithéa and Péfki; *Dive Med (at the Magic Life Club, Plimmíri | tel. 69 55 98 81 02 | divemed.gr)* specialises in diving excursions in the island's south and also offers snorkelling trips departing from Plimmíri harbour.

FISHING

In Greece, anyone is allowed to fish in the sea, although fishing from the coast is rarely successful. It's better to join a ✅ fishing trip, as offered by (for example) *Michális Libéris* in his boat, *Captain Manólis (cost 75–500 euros | tel. 69 41 49 55 39 | captainmanolis. com)*. The round-trip starts from the Kolóna harbour in Rhodes Town, but you can request where to go. Similar offerings are available in all the major resorts on the island. You get to keep your catch, and if you don't catch anything, at least you've enjoyed a day at sea.

HIKING

Rhodes is ideal hiking country. However, there are no proper walking maps and no signposted trails, and hiking guidebooks date quickly. If you want to see the island on foot, you are advised to book a complete hiking holiday with your local travel agency. Guided day trips can be booked with *Outdoor Active (Guide Georgios Katsilis | outdooractive.com)* or *Hiking Rhodes (Gennádi | tel. 69 42 02 92 99 | hikingrhodes.com)*; the latter also offer week-long treks.

HORSE RIDING

A dream destination for horse lovers is *Elpida Ranch* (see p. 73) near Lachaniá. Elpida and Jani have created a small animal paradise here. Elpida offers shorter and longer trail rides with her horses, and multi-day trips with advance booking. Jani looks after old donkeys from Líndos, which you can take for a walk for a donation.

INSIDER TIP
Donkey love

It's best to call ahead and talk about a programme that suits you best.

MOUNTAIN BIKING

For mountain bikers, Rhodes provides ideal terrain. There are plenty of quiet, asphalted roads in the centre of the island and countless more dirt tracks. A particularly good agency that offers guided tours is *Rodos Cycling (Odós Gríva 8, Rhodes New Town | tel. 69 47 30 99 11 | rodoscycling.com). Also located in Rhodes New Town is Fidusa Bike Rental (Odós Th. Sofoúli 97 | tel. 22 41 02 12 64 | rhodosbicyclerental. gr).* For rural rides as well as guided e-bike tours, try *Rhodes Roads (tel. 69 51 79 91 11 | rhodesroads.com).*

Some agencies will deliver bikes to hotels all over the island and to the airport for a fee. The average price is around 15 euros per day and 90 euros per week.

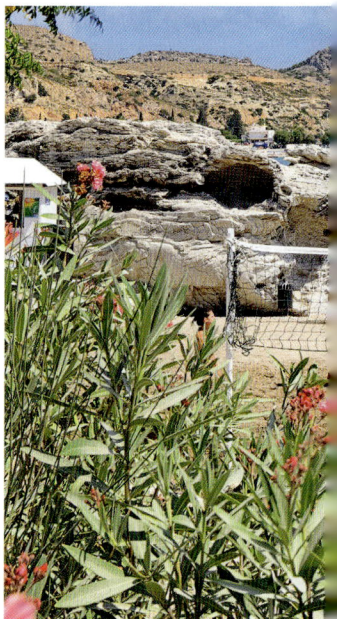

WATER SPORTS

A variety of water sports are on offer on almost all beaches adjoining the larger hotels. Among other activities, you can go waterskiing or sea canoeing, or you can hire a pedalo. The largest selection is available in Faliráki, Kolímbia, Ialissós and Kiotári. You can go banana boat riding or ✅ parasailing without any previous experience. Just leave your mobile phone on land, as you might end up dipping into the water for a moment during your parasailing flight.

The well-protected bay at Líndos is well suited to waterskiing. Stand-up paddleboarding is the speciality of *Paddle Paradise (2hr course 45 euros | north of the beaches | tel. 69 81 56 87 98 | paddleparadise.gr).*

Take part in a variety of activities by, in or on the water, such as here in Stegná

WIND- & KITESURFING

Wind- and kitesurfers like the beaches between Ixiá and Theológos on the west coast the best. There are some busy kite stations in Fánes *(kite-rhodos.com, meltemi-kiteclub.com).*

Windsurfing courses are offered at the *Kiotári Watersports Centre (10 hrs approx. 180 euros | on the beach in front of the hotels Rodos Maris and Rodos Princess, Kiotári | tel. 69 46 45 54 58 | watersports-rhodes.com).* Here you can also get your catamaran sailing licence *(6–8 hrs incl. exam fees: 240 euros)* or windsurfing licence from the International School Association for Water Sports (VDWS).

An ideal spot for experienced wind-surfers is the beach at Prassoníssi in the far south of the island.

In the north of the island in Ixiá is *Windsurfers' World (tel. 69 47 06 22 54 | windsurfersworld.gr)*; the same people also run *Air Riders (tel. 69 44 26 41 00 | kiteprocenter.gr)* in Kremastí. Prices and offers are similar to those at the Kiotári Watersports Centre. The relatively new sport of wing surfing, which uses a wing instead of a sail for added uplift, is also available on Rhodes at *Surfers Paradise (Leofóros Iraklidíou, Ixiá | tel. 69 75 56 43 91 | surfersparadise.gr)* and at Kremásti Beach in Ialissós with *Meltémi Windsurf (tel. 69 44 24 33 10 | meltemi-windsurf-rhodes.com).*

HOLIDAY PLANNER

Mediterranean Sea

THE CENTRE p. 80
Popular bathing resorts, extensive forest and unspoilt countryside

Kritinía

Émbonas

Emborió

Monólithos

LÍNDOS & THE SOUTH p. 58
The beauty queen of the Aegean Sea, plus quiet villages and long beaches

Kattavía

Hike or drive to the southern tip ✓

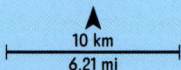

10 km
6.21 mi

✔ On your marks …

✔ Eat at the fish market

Museum of Archaeology ★

Palace of the Grand Master ★

Mandráki Harbour ★

Néa Agorá ★

Old Town ★

Filérimos ★

Kallithéa Springs ★

Rhodes

Ialisós

Take a selfie with an ostrich … ✔

Petaloúdes ★

✔ Go skinny-dipping

Kalithiés

Arhángelos

✔ Join a jungle tour

✔ Discover hidden Rhodes on horseback

Akropolis of Líndos ★

St Mary's Church ★

Líndos

Kiotári

M e d i t e r r a n e a n

S e a

✔ Marco Polo Bucket List

Marco Polo Top Highlights ★

RHODES TOWN

There may be more beautiful cities in the world but none that have such a well-preserved and extensive medieval core. After 2,400 years of uninterrupted settlement, Rhodes Old Town is alive with history. Mosques and minarets, churches and a synagogue show that multiculturalism is not a modern invention; and the 2,000-year-old remains are testimony to monumental architectural achievement in a period when most other Europeans were still living in caves and huts.

The old and the new coexist in the island's capital

Buildings dating from half a millennia ago are now small boutique hotels, bars and tavernas. The streets of the Old Town resemble a bustling bazaar, while the side lanes are populated by more cats than people. Countless yachts are moored in beautiful Mandráki Harbour, while fishing boats and cruise liners dock in front of the mighty city walls. The New Town, with its modern shops and hotels, stretches along two beaches; this is where tourists come to party, while young Greeks prefer to chill out in the Old Town until sunrise.

RHODES TOWN

MARCO POLO HIGHLIGHTS

⭐ **OLD TOWN**
Every stone and every building within the medieval city walls is worth a look ➤ p. 42

⭐ **MUSEUM OF ARCHAEOLOGY**
Ancient treasures displayed in an old medieval hospital ➤ p. 42

⭐ **AVENUE OF THE KNIGHTS**
Follow the cobbled street back to Crusader times ➤ p. 44

⭐ **PALACE OF THE GRAND MASTER**
Quite a sight – whichever way you look at it ➤ p. 44

⭐ **ODÓS SOKRATOÚS**
Named after the famous philosopher, this street in the Old Town is lined with interesting stores ➤ p. 45

⭐ **NÉA AGORÁ**
Get together at the market hall at any time of the day ➤ p. 46

⭐ **MANDRÁKI HARBOUR**
The finest harbour on the entire island ➤ p. 47

⭐ **FILÉRIMOS**
With ancient ruins and a romantic monastery , this mountain offers a bird's-eye view of Rhodes ➤ p. 55

⭐ **KALLITHÉA SPRINGS**
Splash around in the historic ambience of these unique thermal springs ➤ p. 56

The nicest part of the hotel district is "100-palm square" (Platia Charitou).

The party strip – loud and young!

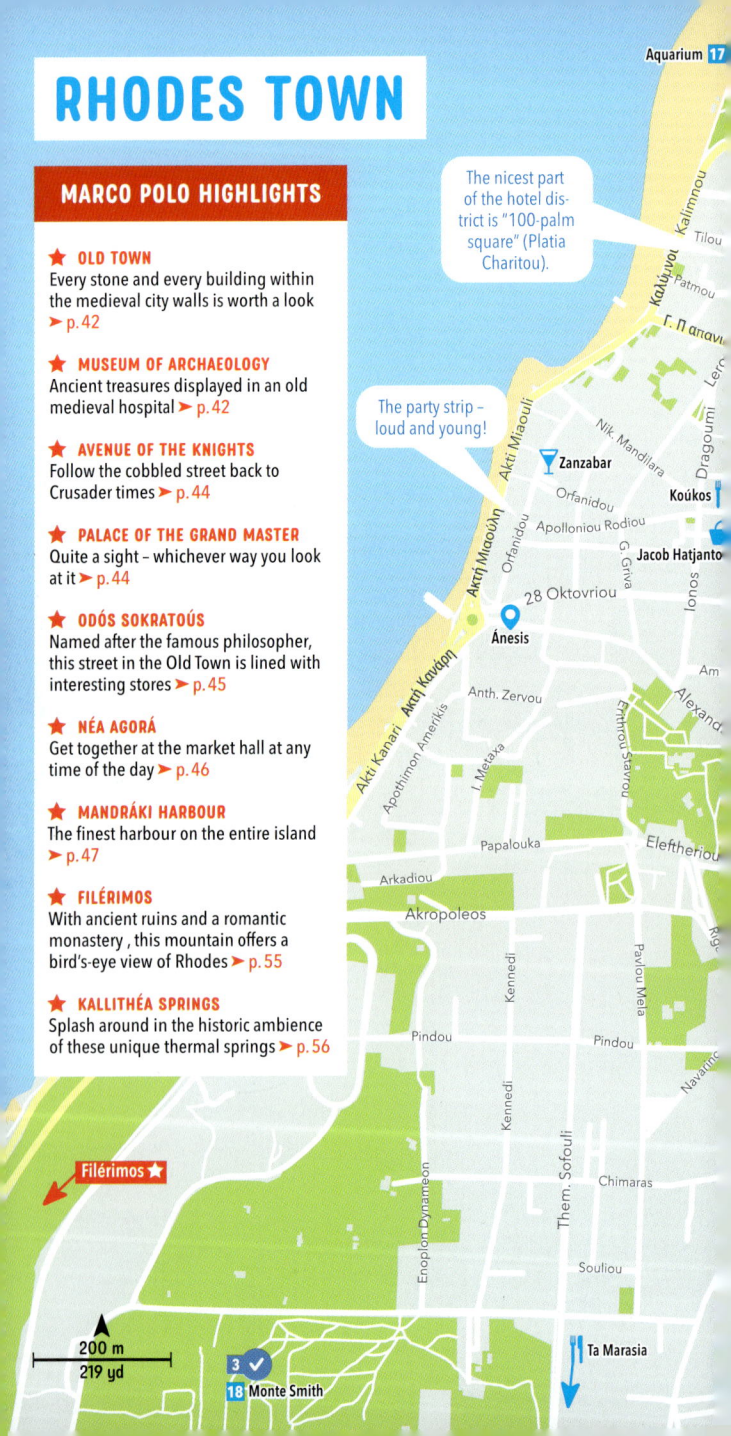

Zanzabar

Koúkos

Jacob Hatjanto

Ánesis

Nik. Mandilara

Orfanidou

Apolloniou Rodiou

G. Griva

28 Oktovriou

Ionos

Am

Alexand

Anth. Zervou

Enthrou Stavrou

I. Metaxa

Apothimon Amerikis

Papalouka

Eleftheriou

Arkadiou

Akropoleos

Pavlou Mela

Kennedi

Pindou

Pindou

Kennedi

Them. Sofouli

Chimaras

Souliou

Naxan

Rig

Enoplon Dynameon

Filérimos ⭐

200 m
219 yd

3 ✓

18 Monte Smith

Ta Marasia

Akti Miaouli

Akti Kanari   Akti Kavadin

Kalimnou

Tilou

Καλίμνου   Patmou

Γ. Π απανι

Lero

Dragoumi

One of the best beaches on the island, and certainly the one with the best bars.

☀ Elli Beach

Elli Beach

Museum for Modern Greek Art

🍸 Casino

N. Savva

G. Papanikolaou

Kathopouli

15 Turkish Cemetery

Polytechniou

I. Efstathíou

7 Martiou 7ης Μαρτίου

Amerikis

Dodekanision

25 Martiou

D. Themeli

Gr. Lampraki

Ethelonton

Εθνάρχου Μακαρίου Gallias

14 Promenade

13 Mandráki Harbour ★

Aktaíon

Platía Kyprou

Γαλλίας,

Averof

Karpathou

Αλ. Παπάγου

Μακαρίου

Etnarchou

Al. Papagou

12 Néa Agorá ★

★ Kontiki Next

2 City walls and moat

16 Museum for Modern Greek Art

Palace of the Grand Master ★ **5**

Psandrou

Ippoton

Avenue of the Knights ★ **4**

Magía Fish Spa

Clock tower

Mama Sofia

Ofeos

6

C

Kamiros Leather

Kaberis

Lachitou

3 Museum of Archaeology ★

Odós Sokratoús (Socrates Street) ★

Socratous Garden

7

Ibiscus

1 Old Town ★ Ακτή Σαχ τούρη

Haris Cotton

Blanc du Nil

Akti Sachtouri

Akti Promitheos

Platía Ariónos

Aghiou Fanouriou

Platonos

Lysippou

Pindarou

Thiseos

8 C

Rhodes by Segway

Ágios Fanoúrios 9

Ippodromou

Ippodromou

10

Platía Doriéos

Walk Inn

Páme Antama

Omirou

Sofokleous

Aristídou

Lysippou

Dimosthenous

Ilkarou

Pythagora

Pindarou

Perikleous

Tarviskou

Gavala

11 Kahal Shalom Synagogue

Kisthiniou

i Park

Dimokratias

9

Kallithéa Springs ★

Aegean Fish 🍴 **4**

The Old Town is a labyrinth, but just stroll around and you'll soon get back to somewhere I recognise.

MARCO POLO BUCKET LIST

3 ✔ On your marks…

There's nothing to stop you sprinting around the ancient stadium on *Monte Smith* – but unlike the original competitors, please wear some clothes ➤ p.49

4 ✔ Eat at the fish market

At *Aegean Fish* you can select your own fish from the market stall and watch it being grilled ➤ p.49

Rhodes' three harbours are not only the island's gateways to the wider world but also great places for fun and exploration. Start at Mandráki.

The island's main shopping district is right here, with top Greek labels plus international brands from Italy, the UK and France. Keep an eye on your wallet!

All the major bus routes for destinations around the island start from the junction behind the Néa Agorá.

SIGHTSEEING

1 OLD TOWN ⭐

The Old Town of Rhodes is a UNESCO World Heritage Site that catapults you back 2,500 years into history. It is impossible to lose your way: the Old Town is fully enclosed by its 4km-long *city wall*. You can either walk on top of the wall or within its 2.5km-long *moat* which skirts the city inland.

The best way to get your bearings around the Old Town is to follow the main streets, and then explore the quieter corners by walking in a zig-zag. Buildings erected by the Byzantines, Crusaders, Jews, Ottoman Turks and Greeks are embedded in the ancient fortifications; there are no new constructions spoiling the view.

Despite its antiquity, holidaymakers from around the world give this city its cosmopolitan flair. It's also fun to watch the world strut its stuff along the cobblestone catwalks in front of the many street cafés and tavernas. *a–f 1–6*

2 CITY WALLS & MOAT

Towering over the city's harbour, the fortifications of Rhodes must have been an intimidating sight to the Turkish soldiers who invaded in 1522. Their mission to conquer the city probably seemed downright impossible. Indeed, the siege lasted six months and the besiegers had to resort to starving the city's inhabitants. The knights finally surrendered and withdrew from the island.

A stroll through the deep, very wide 🐗 moat will give you an impression of the colossal task facing the Ottoman invaders *(main entrances on the Platía Riminis c4 and the Pylí Arkadía e5 | freely accessible).* **INSIDER TIP** **How strong are you?** Try for fun just lifting one of the many stone cannon balls that are lying around. For a change of perspective, climb up onto the city walls *(April–Oct Mon–Fri noon–3pm | admission 2 euros, tickets at the Palace of the Grand Master)* and look down into the moat. Dizzying! Sturdy shoes and surefootedness are essential if you want to walk along the accessible part of the 4km-long wall. Your reward: a great view over the roofs and minarets of the Old Town, which was declared a UNESCO World Heritage Site in 1988. ⊙ *30–60 mins | a–f 2–6*

3 MUSEUM OF ARCHAEOLOGY ⭐

The island's most significant museum lures even the most reluctant visitor to spend more than an hour inside because it is far more than just an exhibition space. Surrounded by

A touch of floral pink here, some sea blue there: the Old Town is extremely photogenic

beautiful gardens and overlooking a large courtyard with a pile of cannon balls and an ancient marble lion, the two-storey building itself is a perfect photo opportunity. Its finest treasure is a small marble Aphrodite statue depicting the goddess with a beautifully sculpted figure. However, the tour begins by following the 28-step open staircase up to the first-floor arcade. Walk through the largest doorway to enter a long, high-ceilinged room that dates back to the 15th century: the sick and the injured were treated in this room by the Knights of St John when the building served as a hospital. The gravestones on the wall are in memory of those who couldn't be saved. A small door leads into the dining halls where two Aphrodite statues stand. There you will also find a tomb stele heralded as a masterpiece of Greek classicism; dating from

around 410 BCE, the stele depicts Krito and Timarista: a young woman mourning the loss of her dead mother.

Continue along a terrace with dolphin sculptures and out into the gardens, where beautiful ancient mosaics are exhibited in an open-air foyer. One of the mosaics depicts a centaur (half horse, half man) returning from the hunt. From the gardens, visitors can visit two other special exhibitions concentrating on Rhodes in the Minoan and Mycenaean period in the second millennium BCE. Stairs lead up to the upper arcade to small side rooms which mainly hold painted ceramics (some with explicit erotic scenes!) found in Rhodes and dating between 500 BCE and 500 CE.

When you leave the museum and turn left, you reach another museum room that is only accessible from the street. This space showcases enormous pottery vessels once used to bury the dead in a squatting position. *Easter–Oct daily 9am–7.40pm, Nov–Easter Wed–Mon 8.30am–3pm; special exhibitions April–Oct only daily 9am–4.50pm | admission 6 euros | Odós Apéllou, Old Town |* ⏱ *1–2 hrs |* 🔲 *c3*

4 AVENUE OF THE KNIGHTS ⭐

Odós Ippotón is the only late medieval residential street in Europe that has remained fully intact. It runs in a perfectly straight line from the hospital of the Order of St John, which now houses the Museum of Archaeology, to the Palace of the Grand Master. To the left and right stand the inns of the various "langues" (or "tongues") of the Order (see Early EU, p. 19), decorated with the heraldic emblems of each Grand Master. The finest emblem belonged to the French knights and stands almost in the centre. *Permanently accessible; building interiors cannot be viewed | Odós Ippotón, Old Town |* 🔲 *b–c3*

5 PALACE OF THE GRAND MASTER ⭐

The most photographed and visited sight in the Old Town is, in fact, a fake. The Italians reconstructed the Palace of the Grand Master of the Knights of Rhodes in the early 1930s to suit the tastes of the megalomaniac dictator Mussolini. It was planned to be his residence if he ever came to live on the island, but he was too busy masterminding wars so stayed in Rome.

In 1856, a bolt of lightning triggered an explosion that blew up the church and turned the original palace into a mass of ruins. Only a few parts of the original structure remain, including the monumental entrance portal with its impressive towers. The building's interior was completely redesigned with ancient mosaics from the island of Kos, solid wood furnishings and Chinese porcelain – elements unknown to the Order of the Knights of St John, whose Grand Master resided here from the late 14th century to 1522. The building lost its importance when the Turks invaded; they used the hospital as an army barracks and prison, the palace's church as a cowshed, and the neighbouring church of the Order as an arsenal.

Ancient mosaics in the Palace of the Grand Master

The ground floor hosts two exhibitions. From a historical perspective, these exhibits are far more valuable than the actual building. One is dedicated to Byzantine Rhodes from the fourth century to 1522. The second, more interesting, exhibit is "Rhodes 2400", showcasing recent archaeological findings. Because archaeologists tend to dig faster than they write, many of these sensational objects have not yet been listed, and therefore cannot be photographed, nor can you buy postcards of them. *April–Oct daily 8am–7.40pm, Nov–March Wed–Mon 8am–2.40pm; special exhibitions April–Oct only, daily 9am–4.40pm; e-tickets for timed slots only available at hhticket.gr | admission 8 euros | Platía Kleovoúlou | ⏱ 2–3 hrs | 🗺 b2*

Navigation aids: the clock tower and the minaret of the Mosque of Suleiman

6 CLOCK TOWER

It is well worth climbing the clock tower to take in the fabulous view over the roofs and towers of the Old Town. *May–Oct Mon–Sat 9am–9pm | admission (incl. a refreshing drink) 5 euros | Odós Orféos 1, Old Town | ⏱ 20 mins | 🗺 b3*

7 ODÓS SOKRATOÚS (SOCRATES STREET) ★

Shopping is on the agenda when you arrive at the main street running through the Old Town. The street climbs gently uphill from Platía Ippokrátous at the bottom to the Mosque of Suleiman at the top. The street is lined on both sides with shops selling all the usual souvenirs and more: jewellery and freshly roasted coffee, leather and furs, natural cosmetics and Greek culinary specialities, kitsch, t-shirts and even lightweight suits of armour. Standing at a slight angle halfway down the street is the tiny *Mehmet Aga Mosque*. **Mevlana Shisha Bar (formerly Bekersir)** at no. 76, the island's oldest coffee house, where you may want to try a traditional hookah, stands diagonally opposite the mosque.

INSIDER TIP
Have a puff

From here, head up the street to the pink-coloured *Mosque of Suleiman* at the top end. Dating from the 19th century, the mosque is not open to the public. Opposite is the tiny 🐘 *Turkish Library (April–Oct Mon–Sat 9am–3pm | free admission | ⏱ 15 mins)* built in the 18th century. The library contains Turkish, Persian and Arabic manuscripts, reminding us that Rhodes was once a cultural and economic centre of the Ottoman Empire. 🕮 *b–d 3–4*

🎱 PLATÍA ARIÓNOS

This tiny square with a mosque and large Turkish baths was a hive of activity in Ottoman times. Today the square comes alive in the evenings when the hipsters of Rhodes meet to party in the many music cafés. *Old Town |* 🕮 *b4*

🎱 ÁGIOS FANOÚRIOS

INSIDER TIP
Saintly assistance

Have you forgotten or lost something? Greeks in this situation call on the help of St Fanoúrios. According to many devout followers, he works better than any lost property office. This ancient church is dedicated to this patron saint of lost belongings and has its origins in the ninth century. Its antiquity can be seen clearly below the ground level of the present structure, which dates back to the Crusader period. With sooty frescoes dating from the 13th to 15th century, you can well imagine how people used to gather here in candlelight. *Open in the daytime | Odós Agíou Fanoúriou |* ⏲ *10–15 mins |* 🕮 *c5*

🎱 PLATÍA DORIÉOS

Three bars and a beautiful fountain can be found on this square. The bars serve mainly salads, burgers and pizzas with views of the *Rejab Pasha Mosque*, which has been waiting over 15 years for a renovation. This is a perfect place for a quiet lunch break. *Old Town |* 🕮 *c5*

🎱 KAHAL SHALOM SYNAGOGUE 🚩

The synagogue, built in 1577 and destroyed by the Germans in 1943, has been renovated and now functions as a Jewish museum and place of worship open to visitors of all religions. Members of the remaining Jewish community are on hand to answer questions. *May–Oct Sun–Fri 10am–3pm | free admission | Odós Dosiádou |* ⏲ *15–30 mins |* 🕮 *e5*

🎱 NÉA AGORÁ ⭐

You cannot overlook this building: it has seven corners, but is only one-and-a-half storeys high. Under the arcades facing the harbour, there are a number of cafés that are busy late into night. Here, you'll find sweets such as *baklavás* and *kataífi*, originally from Turkey and extremely popular on Rhodes. Two kiosks between the cafés

Whatever you're looking for, you'll probably find it at beautiful Mandráki Harbour

sell international newspapers and magazines.

Inside the Néa Agorá stands the former fish-market hall, recognisable only by the fine fish reliefs on the capitals of its columns. Two *kafenía* and several grill restaurants are much in demand, particularly during the day. *Platía Eleftherías Mandráki* | 🗺 *b–c1*

🅱 MANDRÁKI HARBOUR ⭐

The question on everyone's lips is "Where did the famous Colossus of Rhodes once stand?" Legend – and souvenirs – would have you believe it stood astride the entrance to Mandráki Harbour, precisely where two pillars are now erected displaying the island's heraldic animals, the stag and the doe, *elafós* and *elafína*. But divers have actually found remains of its foundation beneath the harbour fortress *Ágios Nikólaos*.

Mandráki is the central hub of the city. Where's the tourist information office? Mandráki. Where's the market? Mandráki. Where do the boats depart from? Mandráki. Translated into English, Mandráki means "small sheepfold". No one knows exactly how the ancient military port of Rhodes Town got its current name. One possible explanation is that the name could have something to do with its physical structure: Mandráki Harbour resembles a pair of pincers and encircles the ships rather like a fold does a herd of sheep. It's well worth a stroll around this picturesque port: the jetty with its three windmills and the harbour fortress – which provides a great opportunity for a selfie with the magnificent Neá Agorá – all date from the 15th century. 🗺 *c1*

14 PROMENADE

The city's ample promenade is called *Eleftherías*, meaning "freedom". Its splendour and beauty unfortunately owe much to the Italian fascists who ruled over the island from 1912 to

15 TURKISH CEMETERY

It may seem like an unlikely place to relax and unwind, but the city's old Turkish cemetery is a perfect retreat. An old

On Monte Smith: a small acropolis with a big view

1943, and whose architectural legacy is still evident today. They erected many classical-style buildings, including the Bank of Greece, the Post Office, the Harbour Master's Office, the Town Hall and the city theatre inside the fortifications, and the Governor's Palace and Bishop's Palace facing the sea. They were also responsible for the construction of the Orthodox *Evangelismós* church *(daily 7am–noon and 5–7.30pm | ⏱ 10 mins)*. Formerly the main church of the Knights of St John, it was reconstructed in 1925 according to old drawings, and its large inside walls are painted in traditional Byzantine style. 🛏 0

Muslim woman, whose children have left the island to work in Turkey, looks after the forlorn cemetery and is always pleased to receive a small donation. The cemetery is in the shady grounds of the tiny *Mosque of Murad Reis*, where you can marvel at the beautiful Ottoman tombstones. *Accessible during the day | access from the Platía Koundourióti, New Town |* ⏱ *15–30 mins |* 🛏 *0*

16 MUSEUM OF MODERN GREEK ART

In the *Art Gallery (Platía Símis 2 |* 🛏 *c2)* and in the *New Art Gallery (Platía Charitou |* 🛏 *0)* there are displays of

Greek art from the 19th and 20th centuries. Rhodes has yet to produce any masters. *Both museums Tue–Sat 9am–2pm | admission 6 euros, valid for both collections | ⊙ 20–30 mins per gallery*

17 AQUARIUM

The delicate proportions of the pavilion make you think of an Art Nouveau café rather than a marine biology institute. As well as a marine biology museum, the basement of the building accommodates the aquarium tanks that are home to fish and other sea creatures from Greek waters, for example, bream, bass, prickly scorpion fish, sea urchin and starfish. *April–Oct daily 9am–8pm, Nov–March until 4pm | admission 6 euros | Kalímnou Lérou | rhodes-aquarium.hcmr.gr | ⊙ 20 mins | ⊞ 0*

18 MONTE SMITH

Like every Greek city with its origins in antiquity, Rhodes Town has its own acropolis. Unfortunately, little remains of its temples. Three-and-a-half columns of a temple dedicated to Apollo make up the sparse remains. A visit to the 110m-tall hill is still worthwhile, however, as you can view the entire town from above: old and new, beautiful and ugly. Its present, rather incongruous name comes from the commander of the British fleet which was stationed on Rhodes in the early 19th century. The Italians later gave the hill the name *Monte Santo Stefano*, which is still occasionally used today. It lies in the west of the town and can be reached easily by bus. A reconstructed

theatre and a partially rebuilt ✓ 👥 stadium are also waiting to be explored. The track is exactly 201m long, and dates back to the second century BCE; it was almost completely reconstructed by the Italians, so how about a sprint? *Permanently accessible via Odós Voríou Ipírou (New Town) | bus No. 5 from Mandráki/Néa Agorá | ⊞ H5*

19 RODINI PARK 👥

The "green lung" of Rhodes Town lies between Monte Smith and the road to Líndos. Above the square, on a plateau, there is a lot to discover: huge ancient plane trees, a watercourse with bridges, peacocks running freely and, in the back, ancient rock tombs. *Freely accessible during the day via Odós Stéfanou Kasoúli or by bus No. 3 from Mandráki | ⊞ H5*

EATING & DRINKING

AEGEAN FISH ✓ 🐖

This taverna by the weekly market serves wonderful fish at very reasonable prices. Choose your fish at the market stall and have it fried or grilled at takeaway prices. Then select side dishes and salads at the excellent self-service buffet and enjoy your food at the tables – beer garden-style. *Tue–Sun 9am–5pm | Odós Klavdíou Pepper 1, on the road to Kallithéa | ⊞ 0*

AKTAÍON 🍴 👥

Housed in the former casino for Italian officers, this café-restaurant with its tree-shaded terrace is publicly-owned by the town and is the meeting place of a cultured local clientele. The location also attracts families with young children due to the childcare facilities at the bouncy castle next door. It has a large selection of cakes to choose from and its tasty dishes are served in large portions. Prices are moderate, since the café depends on its regular customers. *Daily | Platía Eleftherías, New Town | tel. 22 41 07 30 55 | €€ | ▢ 0*

KONTIKI NEXT

Relaxation for your body and soul on board the *Kontiki*, a classy, two-storey floating restaurant located in the Mandráki Harbour. Enjoy a coffee, ice cream, sundowner or dinner accompanied by the sounds of waves. The food is inspired by Mediterranean and Japanese cooking, with both eel and sea urchins on the menu. The view past the ship's mast to the fortifications, Palace of the Grand Master and Néa Agorá is spectacular. *Daily | Mandraki Harbour, New Town | tel. 22 41 03 08 26 | fotisgroup.com | €€€ | ▢ c1*

KOÚKOS

This multi-faceted café-restaurant is also a pub with live music. It looks a bit like the set of a Greek film, with its differently decorated areas, and it offers a variety of food at reasonable prices. Open year-round, this restaurant also has its own bakery where you can buy 🐖 goods to take away. *Daily | Odós Mandilára 20, New Town | tel. 22 41 07 30 22 | €€ | ▢ 0*

MAMA SOFIA 🏴

Mama Sofia, who opened this restaurant in 1967, still runs the kitchen but leaves the rest of the business in the hands of her two sons Stávros and Giánnis, and her grandchildren. Together, they provide excellent and entertaining service as well as delicious food, including succulent steaks, fish and seafood. They also serve a delicacy: *foúskes* or sea squirts. Order one to try it, but one may well be enough! The restaurant also has a small, exclusive wine cellar where wine connoisseur Stávros pours 120 different wines by the glass. He even has bottles of the very exclusive Greek Traminer and Gewürztraminer in his cellar. *Daily | Odós Orféos 28, Old Town | tel. 22 41 02 44 69 | mamasofia.gr | €€-€€€ | ▢ b3*

PÁME ANTAMA

In the early morning, the terrace here is a meeting place for the island's more alternative inhabitants, who come to eat, drink, play games, read and listen to music. The host, Marína, comes from Kárpathos but grew up in the Walloon region of Belgium. Níkos, the chef, is from Rhodes but likes to introduce Asian flavours into his freshly prepared dishes. *Daily | Odós Sofokléous 38, Old Town | tel. 69 45 01 00 98 | FB | € | ▢ d5*

SOCRATOUS GARDEN

Enjoy a relaxing break under palm trees in this splendid garden with its own parrot in the middle of the Old

Socrates Street in the Old Town is perfect for strolling and people-watching

Town. An ideal stopover between all the history for an ice cream or drink served by a friendly, efficient staff. *Open daily | Odós Sokratoús 124, Old Town | tel. 22 41 02 01 53 | €€ | 🕮 b3*

TA MARASIA

This rustic taverna attracts virtually no tourists – but the owner entices his regular customers with freshly made salads, fish and seafood. The *fáva* (pureed chickpeas) with caramelised salmon is absolutely delicious! *Daily from 7pm | Odós Agíou Iánnou 155 | tel. 22 41 03 07 45 | €€ | 🕮 0*

IDER TIP *Fishy favourite*

WALK INN

This pub-like restaurant is frequented all year round by cosmopolitan Rhodians and foreigners living on the island. The pizzas and burgers are excellent, and changing Greek specialities from the kitchen are advertised on the chalkboard. On Sunday afternoons and evenings, you can sometimes listen to live music, from Greek *rembetiko* to rock 'n' roll. *Daily | Platía Doriéos 1, Old Town | tel. 22 41 07 42 93 | € | 🕮 c5*

SHOPPING

BLANC DU NIL

For fans of light, flowing fabrics, this French fashion company, also known as the all-white clothing store, has two stores in the city where you will find an array of white, 100 per cent Egyptian cotton clothing for men and women. *Néa Ágora, near the bus terminal, New Town | 🕮 b1* and *Odós Pindárou/Odós Alchadef, Old Town | 🕮 e4*

Have you seen enough of the town and its museums? Elli Beach and the sea are nearby!

HARIS COTTON

The Athenian designer team of Haris and Eva present two new collections for men and women every year made from cotton and linen. Matching accessories are also provided. *Platía Ippókratous and Odós Sokratoús 59, Old Town | hariscotton.gr | 🕮 d4* and *c4*

IBISCUS 👕

A children's dream: this shop has everything you need to feel like a real knight – from swords and battleaxes to full armour. *Odós Sokratoús 64, Old Town | ibiscusmarket.com | 🕮 b3*

JACOB HATJANTONIS

This shop is full of unique creations at very reasonable prices. Jacob Hatjantonis is a passionate artist who paints sandals, belts, handbags and pebbles he collects from the beach. He finds his new life much more fulfilling than his former job as a food engineer in a world-famous brewery. *Odós Mandilára 20–22, New Town | 🕮 0*

KABERIS

Have you acquired a taste for authentic Greek coffee? You can buy a pack of freshly ground beans in this tiny coffee roastery to take back home. *Odós Sokratoús 77, Old Town | 🕮 c4*

KAMÍROS

Are you looking for locally made-leather goods? Then visit Níkos and Vassílis, who make everything from belts and handbags to sandals in their own shop; they also keep hind leather in their workshop. The shop even has hand-crafted leads which can be personalised. *Odós Sokratoús 175, Old Town | 🕮 b4*

INSIDER TIP
Souvenirs for dog owners

PLATÍA KYPROU

This tiny square abounds with boutiques selling international fashion labels, such as Paul & Shark, Trussardi, Oysho, Versace, Armani, Migato, Diesel and many others. It also has the largest selection of umbrellas in southern Europe. People always wonder why so many umbrellas are sold on an island that sees so much sunny weather. The answer lies in the past when the island was given special tax concessions and umbrellas were far cheaper here than elsewhere. You can also buy a piece of hand luggage to transport your purchases back home. *New Town | 🚇 b1*

SPORT & ACTIVITIES

RHODES BY SEGWAY

If nothing can throw you off balance, jump on a Segway to explore the Old Town. These two-wheel, self-balancing scooters can transport you around the cobbled streets of the city. Escorted by a guide, you can go on a two-hour tour by day or a three-hour tour by night. *65 euros/2 hrs, 85 euros/3 hrs | Odós Ippodamou 37, Old Town | tel. 22 41 11 24 09 | rhodesbysegway.com | 🚇 d4*

BEACHES

The city's beaches are not quiet, off-the-beaten track places. Stretching 400m along the coast, ✦ *Elli Beach (🚇 0)* is the closest beach to Rhodes Town and is located between Mandráki and the Aquarium. The nearest bar is always just a stone's throw away, as is

the water's edge. A 3m-high diving platform is just 20m from the promenade. Paragliders can be spotted gliding over the bay, while the sea is full of paddle boats and waterskiers. The pebbly beach between the aquarium and airport is an alternative on less windy days.

Bathing boats leave Mandráki Harbour for the beaches along the east coast and down to Líndos; or you can reach many of the island's other beaches by bus from Néa Agorá. This makes the island's capital the perfect base for your holiday.

WELLNESS

ÁNESIS

Would you like a massage? This professional salon is frequented by local people. *Mon–Sat 10am–8pm | from approx. 35 euros/hr | Odós Al. Diákou 65, New Town | tel. 22 41 02 03 02 | FB: Anesis-Massage | 🚇 0*

MAGÍA FISH SPA

You can get sore feet walking around Rhodes Town. In the Magía Fish Spa, more than 100 small fish nibble at your hard skin, thereby rejuvenating your feet. You can also get a pedicure and foot massage. *Mon–Sat from 10am | 10 euros for 30 mins | Odós Orféos 20, Old Town | FB | 🚇 b3*

ENTERTAINMENT

Greeks will only frequent the discos and clubs in Rhodes New Town and the holiday resorts if they want to socialise with an international crowd.

AROUND RHODES TOWN

The street party hotspot is *Orfanidou* with its many bars, where it is almost impossible to move. Greek locals prefer to hang out in the Old Town in the evenings, especially in the tiny district between the Ibrahim Pasha Mosque and Platía Ippokrátous *(🔲 d4)*. After midnight, these narrow streets vibrate with sounds coming from the small bars and intimate clubs which also organise live performances. A smaller crowd also gathers at the *Platía Ariónos* in front of the former Turkish baths.

CASINO

Even James Bond would take his dates to the casino in Rhodes Town. The building, which was constructed by the Italian fascists as *Hotel Grande Albergo delle Rose*, looks like a palace. Admission is free and you are not under any obligation to bet. Those who dare and win can take one of the casino's luxury hotel suites on the upper floors. *Gambling tables Mon–Thu 5pm–4am, open continuously from Fri noon until Mon 6am | slot machine casino 24/7 | minimum age 21 | Odós Georgiou Papanikolaou 4, New Town | casinorodos.gr | 🔲 0*

ZANZABAR

The refreshed former Colorado Club is the place to let your hair down. Locals gather here to watch the live performances – Greek rock often features. *Daily from 9.30pm | tickets approx. 10–15 euros incl. the first drink | Odós Orfanídou 57, New Town | FB: ColoradoClubRhodes | 🔲 0*

KRÍTIKA

5km from Rhodes Town / 10 mins by bus

It's not worth a stop, but the single-storey houses lining the coastal road from the airport to the city stand empty and beg the question of what they were originally built for. A tiny mosque provides a clue: when the Turks relinquished Crete in 1898, several hundred Muslims moved to Ottoman-ruled Rhodes and built the town of Krítika. Their descendants later emigrated to Turkey, but the houses still belong to them. 🔲 H5

IXIÁ

6km from Rhodes Town / 10 mins by bus

Package tourism on Rhodes began in this town very close to the island's capital. The Supertower was the Olympic Hotel in the 1970s, where the super-rich shipowner Aristotle Onassis rented a suite. Today, it's very lively here, and windsurfers show off their skills in front of the luxury hotels. You'll find most of the island's surf schools in Ixiá. 🔲 G5

IALISSÓS (TRIÁNDA)

10km from Rhodes Town / 15 mins by bus

Three tourist resorts merged into one: with over 11,000 inhabitants, Triánda,

AROUND RHODES TOWN

Σίμι
Sími

Κρητικά
Kritika

Ρόδος
Rhodes

Mediterranean Sea

Ιαλυσός
Ialysos

Ιξιά
Ixiá

5km, 10 mins

8km, 10 mins

EO95

Ιαλισσός (Triánda)
Ialissós (Triánda)

17km, 12 mins

Σγουρού
Sgourou

Filérimos ★

ΕΛΛΑΔΑ
GREECE

Κοσκινού
Koskinou

Παστίδα
Pastida

2 km
1.24 mi

Kallithéa Springs ★

also known as Ialissós, is not only the island's second largest resort, but together with its neighbour *Ixiá* forms the tourist centre of the west coast. There are a few really good restaurants on the beach.

If you like quaint churches, have a look inside the *Kímisis tis Theotókou Church* in the village centre. It is entirely adorned with well-preserved murals in the traditional Byzantine style. The panels of the iconostasis, which separates the aisle from the altar space, are decorated with seahorses and bare-breasted mermaids. ▣ *G5*

FILÉRIMOS ★

17km from Rhodes Town / 20 mins by car, bus connection only in summer; 5km from Ialissós (Triánda)

Do you have a head for heights and enjoy great views? Then drive up the 267m-tall Filérimos Hill – you can spend a good hour admiring the view from the plateau. You will find yourself in another world, surrounded by the smells of herbs and the buzzing of cicadas in the pines and towering cypress trees.

Restored by the Italians in the 1930s, the tenth century *monastery* has a truly romantic setting, and is popular as a wedding location among local couples. Nestled in green coun-tryside stand the scant remains of the acropolis belonging to the ancient city of *Ialissós*, the ruins of a tiny temple dedicated to the Goddess Athena from the third or second centuries BCE. The foundations of an early Christian

Peach, vanilla, lemon: Sími's pretty ice-cream-coloured waterfront

basilica and several chapels have also been preserved. Easily overlooked at first, the small chapel of Ágios Geórgios Chostós (St George) is set back into the slope; the medieval frescoes inside appear to depict kneeling knights and the eight-point cross of the Knights of St John.

Follow the alley lined with cypress trees to a viewing platform with a cross, from where you are treated to the sight of planes at the nearby airport and a far-reaching view along Rhodes' west coast. As a souvenir, buy a miniature bottle of the herbal liquor Sette Erbe which the monks have been distilling here for centuries. *Excavation sites: May–Oct Tue–Fri 8am–8pm and Sat–Mon until 5pm, Nov–March Tue–Sun 8am–3pm | admission 6 euros, the other paths are freely accessible |* ⏱ *1–2 hrs |* 🏛 *G5*

KALLITHÉA SPRINGS ★

8km from Rhodes Town / 15 mins by bus

Bathe differently: no sand, no beach. This fjord-like bay with gently sloping rock banks offers an alternative destination for sunbathing and swimming, with its relaxing beach bars and sun loungers beneath palm trees, pine trees and parasols. But what catches the eye is the oriental-style dome of the art deco spa building, constructed under Italian rule, following in the footsteps of the Romans who also knew of the benefits of Kallithéa's thermal waters. In the semi-circular main building, between bathing and eating chips, you can look at interesting pictures from the sophisticated era of the 1930s. Arrive early because it fills up very quickly.

INSIDER TIP
The early bi

May–Oct daily 8am–8pm, Nov–April daily 8am–5pm | admission 4 euros, free access to the beach bar after 8pm | kallitheasprings.gr | ⌖ H6

SÍMI

45km from Rhodes Town / 50 mins by catamaran

What an amazing sight! Tourists grab their smartphones and cameras as soon as the ship glides around the cliffs into the harbour of Sími. All three sides of the bay are covered in pastel-coloured houses spilling down the rocky coast. Overlooking the harbour is an elaborate bell tower which crowns the beauty of this idyllic village. At a time when all over Greece picturesque old buildings were torn down for the sake of "progress", to be replaced by faceless concrete blocks, the 2,600 inhabitants of the island of Sími decided instead to renovate their old houses or build new ones in the traditional style. The islanders are reaping the rewards of this wise move to this day: Sími rates as one of the most beautiful islands in the Aegean. In high season, there is a constant stream of boats arriving between 11am and 3pm.

Sími's attractions include the large monastery at *Panormítis*, the upper part of the main village which offers a very beautiful view of the harbour and the small beach at *Pédi*. Should you decide spontaneously to stay over-night, you need only inform the personnel on the ship and ask in one of the hotels or travel agencies at the harbour about a room. The food at the traditional taverna *Diethnés (tel. 22 45*

07 16 74 | €) near the bridge is also good. *Daily boats from Mandráki Harbour; fast catamarans depart from Kolóna Harbour daily | ⌖ 0*

LÍNDOS & THE SOUTH

BEACHES, TEMPLES & MUCH MORE

In summer, the unbelievably beautiful village of Líndos attracts huge crowds of tourists who make their way either on foot or by donkey up to the world-famous acropolis. In contrast, very few holidaymakers set foot in any of the other mountain villages in the island's south. The modern beachside hotels in Kiotári and Plimmíri are mostly all-inclusive affairs.

From the party vibes on the splendid sandy beach in Líndos and the windsurfers in Prassoníssi at the island's most southerly point, to

A view that makes you yearn for the Greek islands: Líndos

the peace of Cape Foúrni and the hippy, laid-back beach bar near Gennádi – Rhodes caters for every taste. The landscape is equally diverse. Monólithos feels like Switzerland by the sea, while the region around Kattaviá resembles the African savannah. Líndos is an archaeological treasure; further south there are only a handful of churches, monasteries and castles to appeal to lovers of history and art. Instead, you can ride on donkeys and horses, spot deer on the roadside and soak up the tranquillity on deserted beaches.

LÍNDOS & THE SOUTH

Κρητηνία
Kritinia

14 Émbonas

The large coach park is evidence that Émbonas is a popular day-trip destination, but if you stay a bit longer you can enjoy local pork from pigs fed on grapes and olives and sample *soúma* alongside the locals.

Atáviros
▲ (1215)

52km, 1 hr 10 mins

Άγιος Ισίδωρος
Aghios Isidoros

Laérma **3**

13 Siána

ΕΛΛΑΔΑ
GREECE

The Old Monólithos ★

● **Monólithos**
p. 74

Ίστριος
Istrios

Προφύλια
Profylia

12 Kap Foúrni

Foúrni Beach

Apolakkiá

25km, 30 mins

7 Asklipic

If luxury and razzmatazz are not a priority for you, then book into a small hotel in Monólithos or Apolakkiá to enjoy simple village life.

p. 74

Αρνίθα
Arnitha

Βάτι
Vati

Kiotár

43km, 40 mins

8 Gennádi

15 Skiádi Monastery

Get off the beaten track in the south of the island. There are large tracts of wilderness, holy monasteries, white chapels and near-deserted villages with a few remaining tavernas.

16 Mesanagrós

📍 **Mojito Beach Bar ★**

9 Lachaniá

5 ✓

17 Kattaviá

10 Plimmíri

The two beaches on the southern tip of the island comprise vast stretches of sand, exposed to strong sea breezes that are perfect for flying kites. But don't forget the sunscreen!

Prassoníssi **18** **6** ✓

Map labels

Μαλώνας
Malonas

Αρχάγγελος
Archangelos

EO95

Μάσαρη
Masari

Χαράκι
Charáki

M e d i t e r r a n e a n

S e a

Κάλαθος
Kalathos

EO95

Vlícha Bay

11

Πυλώνας
Pylonas

Ipsenís

2 Lárdos

Líndos Main Beach

Líndos
p. 62

St. Paul's Bay

Acropolis of Líndos ★

St Mary's Church ★

1 Péfki

5 Glístra Beach

To reach Lindos' top sights, it's best to travel by bus as the car parks are completely full between 10am and 6pm. Evenings are a bit less busy, so spend the day at the beach before you head into town for sightseeing. The same applies to Péfki and Vlícha.

Nearly all the hotels on the Kiotári coast are all-inclusive establishments. The resort has been rebuilt, and nature is returning to the area after the devastating forest fire in 2023. You'll need a hire car to explore.

4 km
2.49 mi

MARCO POLO BUCKET LIST

5 ✓ Discover hidden Rhodes on horseback

At the *Elpida Ranch* you can explore the island's lesser-known landscapes: rocky valleys, forests and meadows ➤ p.73

6 ✓ Hike (or drive) to the island's southern tip

Head over the hill behind *Prassoníssi beach* and you'll get a sea view south towards the coast of Africa ➤ p.78

MARCO POLO HIGHLIGHTS

★ **ACROPOLIS OF LÍNDOS**
The postcard motif of Rhodes – with fabulous views far out to sea ➤ p.62

★ **ST MARY'S CHURCH**
The church in Líndos tells stories like a picture book ➤ p.64

★ **MOJITO BEACH BAR**
A different kind of all-inclusive place: although you pay, a visit here will make your day at the beach exceed your wildest expectations ➤ p.72

★ **THE OLD MONÓLITHOS**
First-class taverna in Monólithos, off the beaten track ➤ p.75

LÍNDOS

(⌨ F11) **Líndos (pop. 800) is the most beguilingly beautiful village on the island. Above the village, the acropolis rock is crowned by an elegant temple behind mighty fortifications.**

The whitewashed village sweeps up the green hillside from two beaches below, with the acropolis on one side and the tomb rocks on the other. Nightlife pulses in the narrow lanes long after the village's 80 donkeys have gone home for a well-earned rest.

SIGHTSEEING

ACROPOLIS OF LÍNDOS ★

By donkey or on foot? It's your choice entirely, but ascend you must if you want to see the most spectacular acropolis outside of Athens.

The way up is well signposted and begins right behind the ticket booth. A tiny terrace overlooking the village's golden sands is the perfect spot to catch your breath and take a photo of a relief carved into stone of an ancient warship. The carving is a tribute by the locals to their Admiral Agesandros, who scared off pirates lurking in the waters around Rhodes at the beginning of the second century BCE.

A steep flight of stairs, with medieval history on your right and ancient history on your left, climbs up to the acropolis from the ship's relief. You then reach the entrance gateway of the Knights of St John. The knights had little time for antiquity and pagan temples, so they basically flattened the ancient relics they found here and

Fragments of the temple on the acropolis, which have been beautifully restored

LÍNDOS

Amphitheatre Club
Rodos-Líndos · Ρόδος-Λίνδος
Elxis Spa
Líndos Main Beach
Mávrikos
Blanc du Nil
Captains' Houses
Líndos by Night
St Mary's Church ★
Kori
Captain's House Bar
Acropolis of Líndos ★
Blue Eye
Lárdos · Λίνδος
Arches Nightclub
Mario's
Yannis Bar
Theatre
Arhontiko
New Gato Bianco
Lardos – Líndos
St. Paul's Bay

Medi-terranean Sea

200 m
219 yd

built their own fortifications. The Danish, Italians and Greeks restored the site over the last century and reconstructed the columns to give a good impression of what the ancient acropolis once looked like. The information boards which display reconstruction drawings help the imagination. When you walk up the wide flight of stairs to the highest plateau, just imagine living in ancient times and making the pilgrimage to the small temple of Athena Lindia, the town's patron goddess. You would only have gained a glimpse of the columns (only some of which have been reconstructed) shortly before reaching the peak because your view would have been obstructed by a colonnaded walkway or stoa, 87m in length and extending across the entire acropolis. The sight must have been enough to take your breath away.

Relax and take in the view overlooking St Paul's Bay, which was the ancient port of Líndos. In year 51, the apostle Paul landed here when he visited Rhodes. The entire village now stretches out below you, offering the perfect aerial photo opportunity. *April–Aug daily 8am–7.30pm, Sept/Oct closing time gradually draws in to 5.30pm, Nov–March Wed–Mon 8.30am–2.40pm | April–Oct admission 12 euros, Nov–March 6 euros, e-tickets*

Luxury homes in the lanes of this picturesque village: the Captains' Houses

for timed slots only available from hhticket.gr | ⏱ 1 hr

CAPTAINS' HOUSES

A halfway decent house in Líndos sells for nothing less than one million euros. These highly priced properties were originally built by Lindian merchants and captains who sailed to all corners of the globe. The carved-relief façades and doors are evidence of their wealth and prosperity. From the inside courtyard, paved with a mosaic of black and white pebbles, you enter the living areas.

The *sála*, the largest room in the house, is always located opposite the entrance. This is where the family slept and where guests were received. The walls of the *sála* were decorated with precious, painted ceramic plates. The oldest were probably brought back by sailors as souvenirs from Turkey; later, potters from Líndos are said to have produced their own, famous "Lindian plates". They were not meant for eating off, but as wall decorations, so they have a recess in the back on which the plate can be hung by a nail. Modern versions are to be had in every ceramics atelier and souvenir shop.

Many of these old architectural gems have been converted into restaurants, shops, holiday homes and hotels, so you may get to experience the inside of one for yourself.

ST MARY'S CHURCH ★

As the legend goes, there was once a devout young man who was so attractive that he was persistently chased by women. However, he wanted to remain celibate so he asked God for his help. In return, God placed a dog's head on the man's head and he was then left alone. This man is known to most as St Christopher, the patron saint of travellers. In **INSIDER TIP A holy dog** St Mary's Church in Líndos (15th century), he is depicted in the bottom row of saints on the right-hand side wall. The other 80 frescoes on the walls and in the dome were painted around 1800 and also tell interesting stories. On the back wall, you can see how the righteous are led by Peter into paradise, and how the sinners are transported by fire into the mouth of a monster where hell's punishment awaits them. More cheerful are the illustrations of the biblical story of Creation in the uppermost rows of images. The pictures here tell how God created the world, the animals and the first man, Adam. The pictures would also have you believe that Eve was made from one of Adam's ribs – something you can discuss in your next coffee break. *Mon–Sat 8am–3pm | admission free | on the main alley |* ⏱ *15–20 mins*

THEATRE

On the lookout for more traces of ancient history? This open-air theatre with a former seating capacity of 2,000 houses the remains of 27 rows of seats and is evidence of the prosperity of this town 2,300 years ago. It lies at the foot of the acropolis rock and provides the perfect backdrop if you are sitting at one of the cafés on the square. ⏱ *5 mins*

EATING & DRINKING

Beauty has a price. Eating out on rooftop terraces and in the courtyards of captains' houses is a little more expensive than elsewhere on the island – but snacks and gyros are also available here at affordable prices.

ARHONTIKO

The best restaurant in Líndos may have relocated to an even more hidden spot, but it's worth seeking out. No matter whether you order langoustines and succulent steaks or just vegetables and stuffed vine leaves, the proprietor Dímitris and his son Sávvas treat all their guests the same. The atmosphere is for everyone to enjoy: tables are set on the roof terrace of a traditional Lindian house,

with a fine view of the illuminated acropolis. *Daily | first alley behind Yannis Bar, on the right | tel. 22 44 03 19 92 | arhontikolindos. com | €€€*

CAPTAIN'S HOUSE BAR

Owner Sávvas dreams of one day leaving his business in the hands of his children and spending the rest of his days fishing. His tiny café bar in front of the old captain's house has a laid-back atmosphere where you can sit and relax while pondering on one of the most richly decorated façades in town. Don't forget to ask if you can see the *sala* with its splendid wooden ceiling at the other end of the courtyard. Sávvas

INSIDER TIP
A beautiful house

The spire of St Mary's Church

speaks excellent English and enjoys chatting with his guests when they stop off for a drink on the way down from the acropolis. *Daily | Odós Akroleos 243 | tel. 22 44 03 12 35 | €€*

MARIO'S

Unpretentious, affordable, popular taverna in the upper part of the village. There may not be a fine view, but this is more than compensated for by the fine Greek food on your plate. *Daily | Odós Agíou Pávlou, on the alley leading down from Yannis Bar | tel. 69 45 42 05 78 | €€*

MÁVRIKOS

The very first fine-dining taverna to open in Líndos is still one of the town's most popular addresses. With views of the beach, acropolis and village, many a celebrity has dined on the restaurant's veranda. The oven-baked lamb as well as all types of fish and seafood are delicious – such as the sea urchin salad or swordfish in caper sauce. *Daily | on the small roundabout at the village entrance | tel. 22 44 03 12 32 | €€€*

INSIDER TIP
Unusual fish and seafood

NEW GATO BIANCO

Looking for the best Italian on Rhodes? Then go no further than the "new white cat" in Líndos. Finest, authentic Italian cuisine, with pizza from the wood-fired oven, served in a traditional setting on a rooftop terrace overlooking the acropolis. Great hospitality and service. *Daily noon–3pm*

and from 6pm | on the square in front of the ancient theatre | tel. 69 34 56 22 53 | €€–€€€*

YANNIS BAR

The only bar in town open all year round from morning to well into the night, and a meeting point for locals and tourists alike. Its small terrace is the perfect spot to watch the village's comings and goings. You may see some locals working "out of office" on their laptops. Small snacks are available 24/7. *Daily | Odós Agíou Pávlou | tel. 22 44 03 12 45 | €€*

SHOPPING

BLANC DU NIL

The white clothing of this international fashion label blends in perfectly in the whitewashed village of Líndos. It could even be used as camouflage. *On the main street to the church*

BLUE EYE

In-vogue Greek fashion designers sell their creations here. Precarious shoes and sandals by Aléxis Tsoúbos, fun summer dresses by Élena Kordáli and extravagant bikinis by Christina Kántova … Come and have fun trying on some new outfits. *On the bypass road*

INSIDER TIP
Buy Greek!

KORI

This boutique brings together accessories and souvenirs from Greek artists and designers "to promote the Greek spirit around the world". *On the main street towards Péfki*

Checklist for St. Paul's Bay: sun, beach, sea!

SPORT & ACTIVITIES

LÍNDOS WATERSPORTS

Lovers of water sports staying in Líndos can head to the station at Pallas Beach or be taken free of charge to the water-sports station in front of the Hotel Lindos Princess on Lárdos Beach. On offer are waterskiing and wakeboarding *(both 40 euros/hr)*, jetskis, motor boats and fun rides. *Tel. 69 44 21 55 80 | thelindoswatersports.com*

BEACHES

Both sandy beaches on large Líndos Bay are beautiful, but pretty crowded: *Líndos Main Beach (also accessible by car)* and the smaller *Pállas Beach (only accessible on foot)*. Both offer water-sports facilities. On the other side of the village, on the heart-shaped *St Paul's Bay (Ágios Pávlos)*, there are two small pebbly, sandy beaches with, unfortunately, exorbitantly high prices for deck chairs.

WELLNESS

ELXIS SPA

The wonderful wellness centre in the first-class *Hotel Lindos Blu*, including its panorama relax lounge, is open to non-residents. In this spa you don't pay for individual treatments; instead you book package deals for between four and ten hours, which allows you to choose your preferred treatments. *Vlícha Beach | tel. 22 44 03 21 10 | lindosblu.gr*

In Thári monastery you can get a glimpse of monastic life

ENTERTAINMENT

AMPHITHEATRE CLUB 🏴

First, it's starry skies, then a laser show, then the sun climbs out of the sea – clubbing à la Líndos. The large open-air club stands high above Líndos Bay with a view of the town and the illuminated acropolis. Good DJs and many live concerts in August. *July/Aug daily 11pm–6am | on the road towards Rhodes Town, 2km out of town | amphitheatrelindos.gr*

ARCHES NIGHTCLUB

Young islanders come to party under the arches of a traditional Lindian house. The club plays funk, house, hip-hop and R'n'B. **The best parties are held on Saturdays, when the local clubbers are at home.** *May–mid-Sept daily from 11.30pm | 10m from the Odós*

INSIDER TIP
Saturdays are best

Agíou Pávlou near the Yannis Bar | archeslindos.com

LÍNDOS BY NIGHT

Classic cocktail bar in the middle of the village. Three floors, a rooftop terrace and green lights that make you feel like you're in a rainforest. You can work up a sweat while dancing between the tables. *Daily 6pm–3am | on the alley that climbs up next to the donkey station | lindosbynight.com*

AROUND LÍNDOS

🬝 PÉFKI

5km from Líndos / 10 mins by car
Péfki is the perfect beach holiday destination. Indeed, the only attraction is its long sandy beach which is divided into

small coves by rocks. There is no old village or any sights beyond the climb to the chapel of *Profítis Ilías* from where there is a beautiful coastal view. The resort is solely geared to the needs of summer holidaymakers with all the usual water-sports stations along the coast, as well as small hotels, restaurants, cafés and bars along the main road. You can walk to Líndos in 90 minutes or explore the island's south by scooter or car.

The best restaurant to enjoy dinner at is the *Ártemis Garden (daily from 6pm | on the main through road | tel. 22 44 04 83 65 | €€)*, where you can also get excellent pizza. At *Tsambíkos (daily from 6pm | below the road to Líndos | tel. 22 44 04 82 40 | €€)* vegetarians will also enjoy themselves; the great food is only topped by a far-reaching view over the town and the sea from the large roof terrace. Later in the evening, *Péfkos by Night (open daily | FB: Pefkosbynight)* is the popular venue in the village centre, playing hits from the 1960s to the latest mainstream pop on its veranda. 🕮 *F11*

2 LÁRDOS

9km from Líndos / 15 mins by car
The small village comes in two parts. *Kafenías* and tavernas serving rustic food cluster around the village square in the old town on the side of the coastal road that faces away from the sea; there is also life in the village during the winter months. History buffs should make the kilometre-long walk from the village square to *Kástro Lárdos*, a fortification that is thought to have predated the Crusaders.

The new Lárdos town is situated 2km away along the beach to Péfki. On the way you pass a small *local heritage museum (daily 9am–3pm | admission 5 euros | ⏱ 15 mins)*, which shows how locals used to live. 🕮 *E11*

3 LÁERMA

22km from Líndos / 30 mins by car
This village lies almost in the centre of the island. There's not much going on, but you can dine well by the village church in *Tákis Taverna Plátanos (May–Nov Tue–Sun from 1pm | tel. 69 84 65 64 76 | €€)*. ==The landlord, Agostinos, bakes and grills Rhodian delicacies with a modern twist.== There is often live music here on Saturdays.

INSIDER TIP
Island cooking 2.0

Head along the tarmac road to the 🐂 *Moní Thári monastery (daily 8am–sunset | accessible with a donation | ⏱ 15 mins)* hidden away in the forest. Enjoy the hospitality of the monks and admire the well-preserved frescoes inside the 14th-century church.

4 IPSENÍS

12km from Líndos / 25 mins by car
The small, white nunnery 5km west of Lárdos is not what you'd call a major attraction in itself. It was built in the 19th century and the bell tower was added in the 1960s. The nuns are hospitable, and the garden exudes a sense of peaceful tranquillity.

==The experience is made more memorable if you climb the gentle slope, following the pilgrims' route past the stations of the==

INSIDER TIP
Food for the soul

cross. *Daily 8am–12.30pm and 4–6.30pm |* 🕮 *E11*

5 GLÍSTRA BEACH

12km from Líndos / 15–20 mins by car

This crescent-shaped sandy beach near Kiotári is backed by four beautiful luxury hotels. It is a popular stop among tourists travelling around the island due to its location directly below the coastal road. Although it suffered in the 2023 forest fires, the local habitat has quickly recovered. 🕮 *E11*

6 KIOTÁRI

16km from Líndos / 25 mins by car

Once the most popoular destination on Rhodes for a relaxing beach holiday, Kiotári was badly hit by the 2023 forest fires. However, almost non-stop construction since means that it can once more offer plentiful holiday accommodation. Since most of the hotels are all-inclusive, the resort has very few tavernas and bars. But these can be found in small villages nearby, such as Lárdos, Gennádi or Lachaniá.

From here, you can also take a speedy motor yacht trip along the east coast to Rhodes Town (50 euros), or to the neighbouring island of Sími (90 euros) with *Kiotari Sea Lines (tel. 22 41 08 50 86 | kiotarisealines.com)*. 🕮 *D11*

7 ASKLIPIÓ

21km from Líndos / 30 mins by car

The original biblical apocalypse is on

Like a biblical graphic novel: St Mary's Church in Asklipió

display in the almost 1,000-year-old *St Mary's Church (⏱ 15–20 mins)* dedicated to the Feast of the Dormition of the Virgin Mary (Assumption) in Asklipió. A devout man in the 17th century painted the scene inside the church; images include the Riders of the Apocalypse and the Antichrist rising from the depths of the Earth. The other walls of the church also resemble a picture book, adorned with saints and scenes from the Old and New Testament.

Right next to the church there are three small *museums (Mon–Sat 9am–7pm, Sun from 10.30am | admission 1.50 euros | ⏱ 15 mins)* which are all worth a visit: the Museum of Sacred Art, containing icons and old liturgical books (Evangeliaria), the Museum of Popular Art with an interesting collection of agricultural implements, and an old olive press.

Opposite the church and museums, you can enjoy authentic Rhodes food in the taverna *Nikóla (open daily | €)*. Try the sausages served with lemon instead of mustard. After a good meal, you should be ready for the short climb up to the signposted castle ruins, from where you are treated to splendid views of the coast and sea. While you are visiting Asklipió, experience a unique kind of cruise by donkey. *Donkey Cruise* is organised by families from the region who rescued a group of older donkeys and gave them a new home. The stronger ones walk with or carry tourists on excursions past old watermills and tiny chapels.

INSIDER TIP
A different kind of cruise

Alternatively, you can just visit the donkeys to feed and stroke them. *Donkey Cruise (from 20 euros as a walker | 200m off the road from Asklipió to Laérma, signposted from there | appointments: tel. 69 44 86 10 56 | donkeycruise.com | ▢ D11)*

8 GENNÁDI

21km from Líndos / 30 mins by car

A lively village where you can stay in small hotels and holiday homes above the coastal road yet in close proximity to the beach. You can also find hotels on the long pebble-sand beach just a kilometre away, where there are also a couple of rustic tavernas.

The village comes alive in the evenings along its small main street, where the sounds from the *Cocoon Lounge & Music Bar* are drowned out by the bass tones from the *Southcoast Music Café* diagonally opposite.

Although you don't have to stop in Gennádi if you're on a tour of the island, one place you must visit is the ★ *Mojito Beach Bar (mid-May–Sept daily round the clock | tel. 69 57 67 26 82 | mojito-beachbar.gr | €)* between Gennádi and Lachaniá. A large sign and pink tractor on the coastal road point the way. Aloe vera grows by the house, which proprietor Andréas and his wife Dóra use for their freshly squeezed juices and special mojitos. Brightly coloured tables and chairs stand outside between the veranda and sea on wooden platforms under the trees. Drinks and snacks are also served to the sun loungers.

If you just want to have a day off and do nothing, the Mojito Beach Bar is the perfect place

Guests can relax in the hammocks or even stay the night in one of the nine cabanas. There is live jazz three times a week, and some of the regular guests even bring their own instruments with them. Twice a week there is a large beach barbecue: once with meat, and once with fish. *D12*

9 LACHANIÁ
30km from Líndos / 40 mins by car
Have you ever dined with a priest before? Although the village taverna *Acropole chez Chrissis (daily | on road to Mesanagrós | tel. 22 44 04 60 32 | €)* officially belongs to his wife, the priest often helps out in the restaurant, peeling potatoes and washing vegetables, and **he is always willing to be photographed in his robes.** Or you can just order a coffee here and then drive down to his village church where right next door is the taverna *Plátanos (daily | tel. 22 44 04 60 27 | €€),* serving some of the island's best Rhodian cuisine.

DER TIP *selfie with the Reverend*

South of Lachaniá, the ✔🐴 *Elpida Ranch (tel. 69 73 39 40 03 | elpida ranch.eu)* is reestablishing itself after staff managed to save its horses and animals from the 2023 forest fires. Elpida offers short and long trail rides through almost untouched landscapes, and there is also the opportunity to pet lots of cute animals or go for a walk with old donkeys from Líndos that Jani and Bernd from *Happy Ears (happyears.org)* have rescued *C13*

10 PLIMMÍRI
35km from Líndos / 45 mins by car
Up until 2015, Plimmíri was a tiny hamlet, home to a harbour, a handful of fish tavernas and a few houses nestled in the surrounding fields. This all changed, however, with the opening of an enormous hotel complex called *Tui Magic Life* in the middle of nowhere. The region has attracted no new businesses or tavernas because the entire hotel village is all-inclusive. However, Plimmíri's long pebbly beach can accommodate many sunbathers and the *fish taverna (daily | plimmirifishrestaurant.com | €€–€€€)* continues to serve authentic, rustic food. The ruins of a monastery (founded in 1837) stand immediately behind the taverna. Plimmíri was a small town 1,500 years ago and many elements of an early Christian basilica were incorporated into its well-preserved *church*. Collecting shells is still a popular pastime on the beach, as are half-day glass-bottom boat rides to *Prassoníssi (40 euros | tel. 69 55 98 81 02 | divemed.gr)*. Boats stop off at the desolate *Paradise Beach* and at a wreck of a traditional *kaíki* boat.

11 VLÍCHA BAY
3km from Líndos / 5 mins by car
Several large hotel complexes are located along the wide 1km-long pebbly beach at Vlícha Bay. Most of the hotels deceivingly incorporate the word Líndos into their names, yet you can't even see Líndos from this bay – and there is no path leading to the idyllic town 3km away. *F10*

APOLAKKIÁ & MONÓLITHOS

(🗺 A–B 10–11) **Rhodes can offer refuge from the masses – the neighbouring mountain villages of Apolakkiá and Monólithos are ideal for this.**

You can stay in small hotels, will quickly get to know the locals and are guaranteed a peaceful night's sleep. Large, by Rhodian standards, the inland village of Apolakkiá (pop. 600), like Monólithos (pop. 330), has only been discovered as a tourist destination in the last few years. Daily life here goes on at a gentle pace as the people make a living largely from the cultivation of cereals, honeydew melons and watermelons.

SIGHTSEEING

ÁGIOS GEÓRGIOS KÁLAMOS ⚑
St George's Chapel, entirely decorated with paintings, has no artistic value, but lies in an idyllic spot above the west coast and offers a panoramic view towards the large neighbouring island of Kárpathos – a good place for a picnic. *Freely accessible | 900m off the road between Apolakkiá and Monólithos; well signposted | ⏱ 10–30 mins*

ÁGIOS GEÓRGIOS VÁRDAS
Do you "collect" churches? This tiny, single-nave church in the woods is important from an art history perspective. Inside, frescos dating back, like the building itself, to the 13th century, remain intact. They depict scenes from the life of Christ and the Virgin Mary. Other figures include St George, to whom the church is dedicated. *Permanently accessible | 1.3km beyond the Platía of Apolakkiá on the road to Monólithos, signposted from the opposite direction and reached via a 2.7km-long dirt road | ⏱ 10–15 mins*

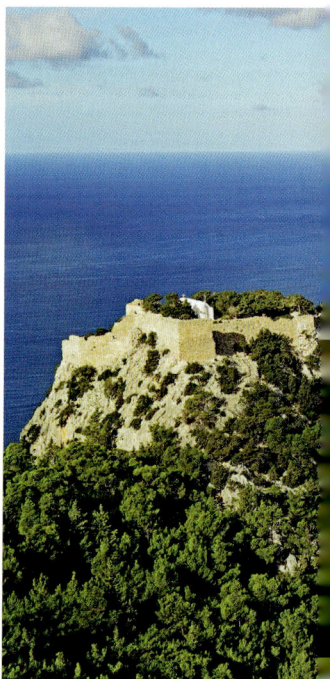

CASTLE RUINS 🐗
The knights built their castles in some truly amazing locations. In Monólithos they chose a gigantic stone finger which towers over the surrounding barren landscape. The way up to the castle is easy though, involving a

There is not much left of the former castle of the Knights of St John on Mount Monólithos

five-minute walk from the road up a rocky path. Only the outer walls, a whitewashed chapel dedicated to St George and a few other ruined buildings have survived.

DER TIP
Stunning sunsets

The best time to enjoy the view across the sea is just before sunset. *Freely accessible | on the road to Cape Foúrni, Monólithos |* ⏱ *40–60 mins*

Africa, and their travels have influenced their cooking. They use only fresh, regional ingredients and all traditional recipes have a refined touch. Their stuffed courgette flowers, which they serve between May and August, are a true delicacy as are, for the more adventurous, the snails which they collect after rainfall. *Open daily | by the village church | Monólithos | tel. 22 46 06 12 76 | €*

EATING & DRINKING

THE OLD MONÓLITHOS ★

The food served here is something special. The proprietors, Manólis and Déspina, lived for a long time in South

BEACHES

You will need a car in order to get to the sea from both villages. The nearest beautiful beaches are at Cape Foúrni.

AROUND APOLAKKIÁ & MONÓLITHOS

12 CAPE FOÚRNI

7km from Monólithos / 15 mins by car

Experience breathtaking scenery on the zig-zag drive down to the Cape. You can clearly mark out the beaches and the Cape from above. A sign on the first of the two beaches, *Alyki Beach*, reads "Please keep it wild", a fitting description also for the beach's tiny bar. Nobody cares how you choose to bathe down here. Just before the road ends at the second beach, the 400m *Foúrni Beach*, you can spot an ancient relief on a rock to the right. It shows the ferryman, Cháron, taking the souls of the dead across the Acheron river to the underworld. What many people don't know: a path (easily walkable with sturdy shoes) criss-crosses the peninsula, leading to ancient graves and a cave church. *A10*

INSIDER TIP
Ancient graves by th sea

13 SIÁNA

5km from Monólithos / 10 mins by car

Swarms of tourist buses stop in Siána on their tour of the island for visits to

Island life has changed little in the villages between Monólithos and Apolakkiá

the huge church, the few nice tavernas and the many stalls selling olive oil, honey, *soúma* liquor and other farm products. *B10*

🔞 ÉMBONAS

21km from Monólithos / 30 mins by car

This large village (pop. 1,200) on the western slopes of the Atáviros (the highest peak on Rhodes) was once one of the most original and authentic on the island. Residents made a living from vineyards, animal husbandry and textile weaving. The vintners and farmers are still here, but in summer the village is flooded with excursion buses.

If you do come, however, visit one of the wineries along the main road – although not necessarily the ultra-modern Emery winery, which is popular with tour-bus groups. Wine tasting here takes place against an industrial backdrop; in the smaller establishments, things are far cosier.

You can eat well at the *butcher-cum-taverna (daily | signposted | tel. 22 46 04 12 47 | €€)* run by the Bákis brothers in the centre of the village. They only use meat from the region, including venison in the winter months. *C8*

🔞 SKIÁDI MONASTERY

10km from Apolakkiá / 15 mins by car

This inland monastery is famous as the place where the icon of the *Panagía Skiadiní* (Mother of God) is kept – when she is not on tour, as she likes to travel. According to local popular

belief, she performs true acts of wonder. The famous icon on the iconostasis cannot be overlooked: silver entirely covers the figures of the Virgin Mary and the Baby Jesus, except for their face and neck. Many votive offerings are placed near them.

In the weeks leading up to Easter, the Virgin is brought for one or more days to the surrounding villages according to a strictly regulated plan by which the icon stays in the church or the private houses of generously donating locals. This is supposed to give the entire community God's blessing. Ascetic visitors can also spend a night in one of the monastery's basic yet clean cells *(donations welcome)* in the summer. The sunset from here is spectacular and well worth the walk up. *On the tarmac road from the west coast to Mesanagrós | ⏱ 20–30 mins | B12*

INSIDER TIP
A night in the monastery

🔞 MESANAGRÓS 🚩

14km from Apolakkiá / 20 mins by car

The clocks must have stopped here around the end of World War II. The 30 or so inhabitants of the village in the Koukoúliari hills still live in traditional one-room houses. Young people are a rare sight, most of them having moved to Rhodes Town or to one of the holiday destinations on the east coast.

The elderly remain, and are delighted with anyone who has a little time to spare and sits down for a chat at the little coffee house, the *Village Café (Tue–Sun | €)*. The café

Prassoníssi in the island's far south is a kitesurfer's paradise

owner also has the key to open the medieval *church* opposite, which shares many architectural features with early Christian basilicas. An ancient column is used as a door lintel, while colourful mosaic remains dating from 500 BCE decorate the courtyard. A small but modern *museum* displays many archaeological artefacts from the region.

Some 3.5km to the south, on the road to Lachaniá, is the tiny *Ágios Thomás* church. His feast day is "Thomas Sunday", the Sunday after Easter, when a popular, bustling parish fair is held under the old cypress trees in front of the church, with picnics, music and dancing. ▥ *B12*

17 KATTAVIÁ

17km from Apolakkiá / 15 mins by car
A poor, almost downtrodden village that nevertheless has an authentic charm: the *platía* is nothing more than a widening in the road covered in old tarmac. Around the square stand four, usually empty, tavernas. The prettiest of then is the *Taverne Penelope (daily | €)*, resembling a village museum. The best food is cooked by Eftichía and her sons Dimítris and Theodóris in 🐄 *Eftichía (open daily | tel. 69 44 79 43 42 | €)*. The village stands on a plateau. The surrounding landscape bursts with colour in spring, only to dry out in summer to resemble the African savannah. Head off the main road towards the east coast and you will see the impressive ruins of a large old silk factory standing isolated on your right-hand side. The bell tower of the *Agios Márkos* church stands on your left towering over the old cowsheds next door: before the war, Kattaviá was the centre of the island's dairy production. ▥ *B13*

18 PRASSONÍSSI ⊘

25km from Apolakkiá / 20 mins by car
Speed, waves and strong winds

SLEEP WELL IN LÍNDOS & THE SOUTH

COUNTLESS ACTIVITIES

The place for anyone who wants to be active and sociable: in the evening, the taverna of young landlord Thomás is the hang-out spot in Monólithos village. Thomás welcomes all of his overnight guests with a glass of Rhodian *soúma* and marinated fruit. He also helps to plan mountain bike tours and hikes, jeep tours and wine tastings. Furthermore, he can get you access to the local telescope, where you can track shooting stars with the experts. You'll wish you could extend your stay. *Thomás (Monólithos, in the old village street | tel. 22 46 06 12 91 | thomashotel.gr | 10 rooms | €–€€)*

TREAT YOURSELF!

Experience pure luxury with stunning views for 250–700 euros per suite between the village and the acropolis of Líndos. This historic house contains many precious items from centuries past, and the garden is just wonderful. When building the house, the owners followed a sustainable approach, using predominantly regional and natural materials. All fabrics are made from natural fibres, the bathrooms have organic cosmetics and the waste is separated for recycling. Treat yourself in the *Mélenos Líndos (Odós Akropoléos | tel. 22 44 03 22 22 | melenoslindos.com | 12 rooms | €€€).*

– kite- and windsurfers rave about the conditions on this sandy beach, stretching around the island's southern tip. Winds of up to 50kmh are reached in high summer, with waves over 2m high on the eastern side. A paradise for professionals, but beginners should steer well clear. There are three surf centres based in the far south which also organise parties in summer.

Non-surfers can enjoy the view out to sea, hire sun loungers and swim in the designated bathing zone to the east. There are two hostels and three tavernas. The road from Kattaviá to Prassoníssi leads through a Greek army tank training area – the tracks are impossible to miss. This area is a restricted zone. On foot or by scooter you can discover two small beaches on the east coast and also the southernmost point of Rhodes with a view of the island of Karpathos. *B14*

THE CENTRE

Rhodes is chameleon in character, changing its appearance constantly as you drive across it. The island's central section is a place of jarring contrasts, as well as more subtle variations.

The fertility-bringing hilltop chapel of Tsambíka and the hotel high-rises in Faliráki stand worlds apart. The eucalyptus avenue that leads into Kolímbia is evidence of meticulous planning, while the maze of old streets in Archángelos suggests a more chaotic side to the island. Unspoilt Tsambíka Beach is almost like a mini Sahara

Holiday soundtrack in Ladikó Cove: waves splashing against the boat

desert by the sea, whereas Profítis Ilías has forested slopes and an Alpine chalet. A visit to the verdant Butterfly Valley can be combined with a short horse ride through a vineyard.

History has left behind a wealth of attractions in this region. Travel back in time on a stroll through the ancient town of Kámiros. Practise your chivalry in one of the castles and be witness to a sad family drama in a tiny Byzantine church. Feeling hungry? Then enjoy fresh fish in Kámiros Skála or the best pizza on the island in Afántou.

THE CENTRE

MARCO POLO BUCKET LIST

7 ✓ Go skinny-dipping!

You have to try it once in your life, so why not at *Mandomata Beach* near Faliráki? ➤ p. 85

8 ✓ Take a selfie with an ostrich

… and then eat a huge fried ostrich egg for lunch at the *Farma of Rhodes* animal farm ➤ p. 89

9 ✓ Join a jungle tour

Drink coffee, walk and cook on an informative and entertaining tour with *Níkos Pápas*, as he reveals his island home ➤ p. 94

The coast around Kámiros is a slice of rural Rhodes, with small hotels near the beach and good-quality fish taverns.

37km, 40 mins

Σορωνή
Soroni

Φάνες
Fanes

Καλαβάρδα
Kalavarda

● **Kámiros** ★
p. 96

Σάλακος
Salakos

Δίμυλ
Dimyl

18 Chálki ⇐

Μανδρικό
Mandriko

16 Kámiros Skála

17 Kastro Kritínias

Κρητηνία
Kritinia

Profítis Ilías ★ **12**

Άγιος Νικόλαος
Fountoúkli **11**

Απόλλωνα
Apollona

G R E E C

The second-highest mountain range on Rhodes can be explored by car and on foot. Wander in the shade of pine trees to peaceful villages with old-style taverns.

MARCO POLO HIGHLIGHTS

★ **PETALOÚDES (BUTTERFLY VALLEY)**
At its most beautiful in the butterfly mating season of July/August, but always a green oasis ➤ p. 88

★ **PROFÍTIS ILÍAS**
Have you come to the wrong place? Coffee and cakes up in the clouds, with architecture and forest just like in the Alps ➤ p. 93

★ **KÁMIROS**
A great trio: ancient town, good beach and tasty food ➤ p. 96

Λάερμα
Laerma

Ρόδος
Rhodes

Ιαλυσός
Ialysos

Κρεμαστή
Kremasti

Σγουρού
Sgourou

Παστίδα
Pastida

Koskinoú **2**

Δαματριά
Damatria

5 Vineyard Triantáfillou

Μαριτσά
Maritsa

6 Farma of Rhodes
8 ✓

Faliráki
p. 84

4 Petaloúdes (Butterfly Valley) ★

Καλυθιές
Kalythies

Mandomata
Beach **7** ✓

Anthony Quinn Bay **1**

3 Psínthos

Afántou
p. 87

7 Katholikí Afántou

Visit Petaloúdes and Psínthos to experience the island's forest land-scapes at their most beautiful – and to sample the best of Rhodian cuisine.

20 km / 45 mins

10 Archípolis

9 Eptá Pigés

Kolímbia
p. 90

Tsambíka
Beach

8 Tsambíka

Holiday central. There's little wind here so it's very pleasant in May and October, but very hot in August. Faliráki is loud and youthful, Afántou is more isolated and traditional, while Kolímbia is tranquil and luxurious. From all three, it's easy to reach the must-visit destinations of Rhodes Town and Líndos.

Μαλώνας
Malonas

9 ✓

Archángelos
p. 93

13 Stegná

ΛΑΔΑ

Μάσαρη
Masari

Tradition and tourism both thrive in the appealing town of Archángelos – it's beautiful and still full of local life. There are beaches nearby at Stegná and Charáki.

Charáki **14**

15 Féraklos Fortress

4 km
2.49 mi

Faliráki is the party capital of Rhodes

FALIRÁKI

(◫ H6) **Faliráki is a bustling hive of activity between June and September. The wide, sandy beach stretches for 4km and the island's capital is just ten minutes away by bus – no wonder that the town attracts so many tourists.**

Travel operators have no difficulty finding accommodation for tourists in Faliráki; the town is full to bursting with large hotels. Most of the major complexes line the northern end of the beach, while the resort's south is the island's entertainment capital, with no end of pubs, sport bars and nightclubs, and a few striptease clubs interspersed with stores appropriately named "Alcohol World", as well as pharmacies open 24/7. The tiny harbour in the south hints at the former simplicity of this old fishing village, and is where authentic Greek tavernas can still be found. If you continue along this road, you will come to the island's only official nudist beach and a café for stargazers. The resort offers a diverse mixture of attractions to suit most tastes: you are free to decide what you want to do and what you prefer to avoid.

EATING & DRINKING

AKTÍ 🐗

Mama Paraskeví and her son Nektários remain completely unfazed by the hustle and bustle of the tourist masses. They run their small taverna at the harbour entrance in the traditional Greek manner – with warmth and dedication

– and prefer to serve up no-frills, honest-to-goodness fare. Here you are welcome to order just a pint of beer – for less than 3 euros. *Daily | tel. 22 41 08 66 32 | €*

INSIDER TIP **Cheap beer**

STÁMA 🐷

The proprietors of this small taverna have their own fishing boat and offer their catch exclusively here.

INSIDER TIP **Eaten whole**

The sardine-sized *gópes* are usually on the menu – a delicious and simple freshly fried treat. The fine Greek salad is accompanied by the leaves and twigs of the caper bush – including thorns – marinated in vinegar. Believe it or not, these are not only edible, but extremely tasty. *Daily | at the fishing harbour | tel. 22 44 08 64 95 | €€*

STÉFANOS

Among the beach tavernas in front of the gigantic hotels of Faliráki, this one is the best. It is still run by a local family, and the menu includes a large variety of dishes and regional specialities. *Daily | Odós Apollónos, next to Hotel Apollo Blu | tel. 22 41 08 51 65 | €€*

SHOPPING

There are a host of small supermarkets and souvenir shops, but little else.

SPORT & ACTIVITIES

All kinds of water sports are offered by the big hotels on the main beach. Speedboats up to 30hp can be hired in the harbour even if you don't have a boating licence.

FALIRÁKI WATER PARK 👬

This facility on the coast road towards Kallithéa is one of the biggest water parks in Europe. *Daily June–Aug 10am–7pm, May and Sept/Oct until 6pm | admission 27 euros, children (aged 3–12) 19 euros | water-park.gr*

BEACHES

At more than 4km long and up to 50m wide, Faliráki's main beach extends from the big hotels in the north of the village to the small harbour close to the centre. Either side of this, there are a number of other beaches and rocky coves which you can reach quickly on foot or by bicycle.

If you are not bothered by a rocky coastline with stones beneath your feet when in the water, or if you have packed water shoes, it's worth walking around 700–1,300m from the northern edge of Faliráki, away from the road leading to the thermal spas of Kallithéa, to get to the lovely coves of *Nicólas Beach*, *Tássos Beach*, *Oásis Beach* and *Jordan Beach*. Each beach has a small beach bar and sun loungers along the flat rock plateaus and stony pools. The official ✅ 🏊 *Mandomata Nudist Beach* is at the southern end of the bay, where umbrellas and sun loungers can be hired.

ENTERTAINMENT

Ermou Street, the short street that ends at the main square on the seafront, is the main bar and club strip in Faliráki. It's relatively calm during the day but transforms into a party zone when night falls. *The Mix Club (June–early Oct daily from midnight | Faliraki Shopping Center | @mixclub faliraki)* churns out dance music until the morning.

ASTRONOMY CAFÉ

Outer space is within touching distance at Stergio's place. Here, you are surrounded by the symbols and myths of the constellations. And, of course, the cocktails are simply out of this world! *Mon–Sat from 8pm 20, but double-check | Profítis Amos | tel. 22 41 08 61 12 | astronomy cafe.gr*

AROUND FALIRÁKI

1 ANTHONY QUINN BAY
3km from Faliráki / 10 mins by boat

This small, rocky cove near Ladikó got its name because the Greek military junta presented it as a gift to the famous actor – in recognition of the fact that it was here in 1961 that he shot the film *The Guns of Navarone* and therefore introduced the island to millions of movie-goers all over the world. The democratically elected government later reclaimed the land, and it is now accessible to all. *On the coastal road in the direction of Líndos, turn left after 1km towards Ladikó;*

The beach at Anthony Quinn Bay has Hollywood appeal

diagonally opposite the Hotel Ladikó, a dirt road leads to the bay | 🗺 H7

2 KOSKINOÚ

7km from Faliráki / 15 mins by car

A traditional Greek village close to Faliráki. The taxi ride to Koskinoú costs just 10 euros and it's worth the trip for the village's maze of narrow lanes with small houses and old mansions. A 20-minute circular walk through the village begins at the church and leads past the local museum in a typical old residence, as well as the good taverna *O Giánnis (daily | tel. 22 41 06 35 47 | €)*. Head left from the restaurant and then go left again to get back to the village square beneath the church. It's best to come in the afternoon when the tavernas open. 🗺 H6

AFÁNTOU

(🗺 G7) **Afántou is not pretty but it is real, which is why many of its guests come back year after year.**

They crowd the pavements and the maze of one-way streets, which are virtually devoid of parking spaces, undisturbed by the architectural mayhem surrounding them and the fact that there are no views of the sea from Afántou. They take pleasure in the town's bustling authenticity, know the locals and even have Greek friends. After a day spent on the long stretch of sandy beach, the locals and tourists all come together in the town's many tavernas and coffee houses.

EATING & DRINKING

FOUR SEASONS

This stylishly modern bar serves ample portions of pizza and pasta, and the mixed grill is pretty huge. Regular guests order the *kléftiko*, succulent lamb cooked with potatoes and vegetables in a tomato sauce with feta, which comes fresh from the oven at 6pm every day. *Daily | Pernou, on main street towards the beach | tel. 22 41 05 19 90 | €*

INSIDER TIP
A Rhodian staple

O THIÓRIS

Looking for a snack to satisfy your hunger? Then head to this traditional white and blue taverna, where the Greek proprietor Theó will inform you what the kitchen has on offer today.

Do as the locals do and order a little of everything. Sit in summer under the shady trees, and in winter next to the open fireplace. *Daily from 8pm | Odós El. Venizélou | near the Family supermarket | tel. 22 41 05 33 40 | €*

SERGIO'S

Fancy a pizza? Here, you can get a huge wood-fired one with delicious toppings. You can even order takeaway to be delivered to your apartment. *Daily from 1pm | 20m from the main square | tel. 22 41 05 20 50 | €*

BEACHES

The sand and pebble *Afántou Beach* is 60m wide and 4km long. It offers almost no shade at all, but there are a few kiosks serving snacks and a few deck chairs. Once an hour in the daytime, a 🚃 miniature train on wheels (ride: 5 euros) plies the route from the village square to the beach.

AROUND AFÁNTOU

🖪 PSÍNTHOS

8km from Afántou / 40 mins by bicycle

Psínthos is the place to go for a rural dinner. For the Rhodians, the inland village surrounded by green is a historical location. It was here that the Italians defeated the Turks in 1912 and brought the island under their control. It took more than another 30 years for the island to become Greek, after the end of World War II.

On the edge of the village, you can dine year-round in pleasant, rustic surroundings at the *Artemída House (daily | tel. 22 41 05 00 03 | tavern artemida.gr | €)* on the road to Archípolis. The regional delicacy of stuffed kid, roasted over laurel wood for 12 hours, is delicious, as is the roast leg of pork. Salads and vegetables are from the owners' garden or from nearby farmer friends. 🕮 *F7*

🖪 PETALOÚDES (BUTTERFLY VALLEY) ⭐

16km from Afántou / 25 mins by car

A good choice! Between June and August, hundreds of thousands of butterflies (in Greek *petaloúdes*) populate 5km of this lush, green valley. Usually, they sit with their wings closed, quite inconspicuous, on the leaves of the sweet gum tree; at other times they fill the air – and sometimes the kitchen of the taverna – in dense swarms! The insect in question is in fact a moth, with black front wings and glowing orange back wings: *Panaxia quadripunctaria* – or Jersey Tiger, to give it its English name.

The beautiful countryside is worth a visit at any time of the year. It has a small *Natural History Museum (only May–Oct | visit included in the admission to the valley)* with a butterfly collection and an idyllic taverna *(butterfliesrestaurant.gr | €).* INSIDER TIP **Perfect past** The spaghetti served by proprietor Dímitri is top class, as is the moussaká, freshly made every day. *Mid-June–mid-Sept*

Petaloúdes – speed dating for butterflies

daily 9am–6pm, otherwise until sunset | admission mid-June–mid-Sept 5 euros, May–mid-June and mid-Sept–Oct 3 euros, Nov–April free admission | ⏱ *1–2 hrs |* 🗺 *F6*

5 TRIANTÁFYLLOU

19km from Afántou / 30 mins by car

Anastasía Triantáfyllou, daughter of the vinicultural dynasty Emery, is a passionate wine grower. She is almost always to be encountered in this winery, established in 1995 on the main road along the west coast to Butterfly Valley. She sells homemade wines (which customers can taste before buying) and the distilled spirit *soúma*, as well as olive oils and marinated olives. There is also a wide selection of natural Greek products including soap made from donkey's milk, mastic gum oil or black volcanic ash. On

Thursdays, or by appointment, Anastasia's son Jáson, who studied viticulture in Bordeaux, invites guests to join him at the vineyard *(entrance/driveway is 100m before Farma of Rhodes).* Visitors are welcome to tour the vineyard and taste all wines, served with accompanying snacks, while the wine producer talks about his ambitious aims for the vineyard, in French or English. The view over the vines stretches to the Profítis Ilías mountain. *Open during the day | tel. 69 73 42 37 68 | estateanastasia.com |* 🗺 *F6*

INSIDER TIP
Meet the wine grower

6 FARMA OF RHODES ✔ 👶

19km from Afántou / 30 mins by car

This private animal park offers an interactive experience: you may stroke and feed most of the animals,

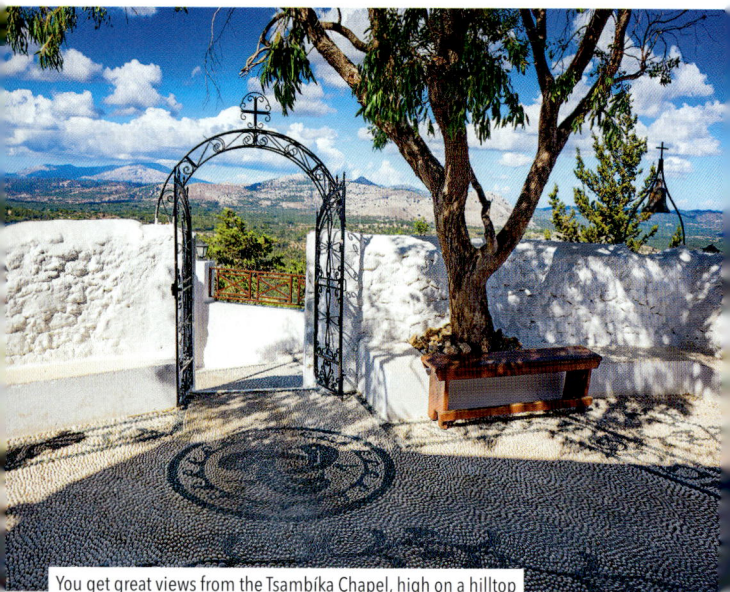

You get great views from the Tsambíka Chapel, high on a hilltop

and most will stand still for a selfie. There are dromedaries, llamas, wild boars, deer, sheep, goats and many ostriches. The park's taverna serves ostrich omelettes and meat; the shop sells colourfully painted ostrich eggs, as well as creams and oils made from ostrich fat. *Daily 9am–5.30pm | admission: adults 17 euros, children (aged 3–12) 12 euros, discounts available online | well signposted on the west coast road to the butterfly valley | farmarhodes.com |* ⏱ *1–1.5 hrs |* ▥ *E6*

⁷ KATHOLIKÍ AFÁNTOU

2km from Afántou / 30 mins on foot
Building work on the small church, which is located within the ruins of a much larger church dating from early Christian times, continued on and off for many centuries. It is worth a visit,

above all for the frescos – the images of boats are particularly striking. To reach the church, you have to drive past the village, coming from the direction of Rhodes Town. Shortly after the signpost which reads "Afántou Golf" there is a sign for Afántou Beach – turn off here. The church is situated on the left. ⏱ *10–15 mins |* ▥ *G7*

KOLÍMBIA

(▥ G8) **A 2km-long road lined with eucalyptus trees leads you into the town of Kolímbia. With over 40 hotels – most of which are all-inclusive – the resort competes with Faliráki and Ixiá, yet it has its own distinctive charm.**

Most of the hotels are pleasantly spacious, low-rise complexes set a good distance apart. The town only has a few (long) streets, all named after European capitals, and you will find no loud clubs or bars anywhere.

EATING & DRINKING

TO NISÁKI

The name translates as "small island" and this taverna is dedicated to fish. Most of what the proprietor puts on the tables comes from the Aegean. Next door, he also runs a bar, and the whole set-up is just a few steps from the beach. *Open daily | at the northern edge of town | tel. 22 41 05 63 60 | €€€*

SPORT & ACTIVITIES

On the main beach north of the village centre *Kolymbia Watersports (tel. 69 37 11 14 61 | kolymbiawatersports. com)* has jetskis and speedboats which you can rent without a boating licence. They're a good way to explore the many beaches along the east coast between Faliráki and Líndos.

BEACHES

The beach, which is windy here, is not one long stretch of sand, but is divided into two coves which gives it a much more intimate feel than the beach at Faliráki, for example.

AROUND KOLÍMBIA

8 TSAMBÍKA 🐾

5km from Kolímbia / 15 mins by car plus a further 10 mins on foot

If you meet somewhere in the world a man named Tsambíko or a woman named Tsambíka, you will know where they come from: Rhodes. And you will also know who was responsible for their conception. The tiny white-washed monastery church on the mountain peak (🕐 *1-hr return trip)* is a place of pilgrimage to this day and is visited in particular by young women in the hope of children. While most tourists drive up half the way, female pilgrims crawl up to pray for fertility and the chance of a child. It is said that the pilgrimage will be most fruitful if the pilgrim shoulders a sack containing a heavy stone.

A path leads through a white gateway into the monastery courtyard. Women enter their name and their wish in the thick guestbook lying open in the chamber on the right. On the left-hand side there is an empty chamber which serves pilgrims as a dormitory. Tsambíka's miracle-working icon of the Virgin Mary is only visible in the church on 7 and 8 November. For security reasons, she stands for the rest of the year in the modern monastery *Káto Tsambíka*, located on the main road to Líndos, just 1km away from the road up to the hilltop chapel.

Between the old and the new monastery, a lane branches off to the unspoilt 🏖 Tsambíka Beach. The sand is so fine that storms have heaved it against a slope at the southern edge of the bay, where it resembles a high dune in a desert. The tourist facilities, on the other hand, are anything but barren: improvised beach bars, sun loungers and a water-sports station provide entertainment for all ages. 📖 *G8*

9 EPTÁ PIGÉS 💆

6km from Kolímbia / 15 mins by car

It is always pleasantly cool under the huge sycamore trees in the valley of Eptá Pigés ("Seven Springs"). The

If you are longing for a cool place, visit Eptá Pigés

many peacocks seem to like the environment, too. The feature that attracts visitors to this popular destination is a 186m-long underground water channel dug during the Italian occupation of the island, which you can wade through. At the end of the tunnel is a pond set amid a gently rolling, lush green landscape. Walk over the hill above the tunnel to get to this idyllic spot. A word of warning: since the whole area is a protected source of drinking water, you will have to do without taking a dip in the pond.

Directly behind the car park, you'll find the taverna *Seven Springs (daily | tel. 22 41 05 62 59 | €)*, where you can order simple Greek dishes such as *souflák i* (meat grilled on a skewer) or *paidákia* (lamb chops). 📖 *G8*

10 ARCHÍPOLIS

10km from Kolímbia / 20 mins by car

A different kind of treehouse: the ancient *sycamore tree* in front of the stairs to the *Ágios Nektários* monastery, near the inland village Archípolos, can fit an entire family inside its completely hollowed-out trunk. The 🧸💆 *Toy Museum (Tue–Sun 10am–4pm | admission free | toymuseum.gr | ⏱ 30-40 mins)* on the road towards Psínthos offers more fun for young and old, as you can try out many of the games from all over the world, as well as looking at them. 📖 *F8*

11 ÁGIOS NIKÓLAOS FOUNTOÚKLI

16km from Kolímbia / 25 mins by car

There are no house to be seen around here, just low-lying rocks and green countryside, but a 600-year-old church stands on the roadside where goats and sheep sometimes congregate in front of the fountain and fruit producers sell their goods: a splendid spot for a small picnic.

Founded by a high-ranking Byzantine official, the church was also the setting for a family tragedy. The official and his wife are depicted on a fresco next to the west entrance. On the opposite wall, the couple's three children are represented. An inscription relates that they all died at around the same time, probably as a result of some kind of epidemic. ◷ *15–20 mins | ◫ E7–8*

12 PROFÍTIS ILÍAS ⭐

20km from Kolímbia / 35 mins by car
Are temperatures getting too hot? Then ride up to the island's second highest mountain. At a height of almost 800m, it is pleasant up here even in summer; islanders come to the forest with their children mainly at the weekends. The Italians built the hotel *Élafos (tel. 22 41 04 48 08 | elafoshotel.gr | €€)* (see p.99) up here in 1929 in the style of an Alpine chalet. Its café serves delicious cakes and desserts. In order to work off those calories, you can hike along the forest paths (ask at the hotel for a map). Only the summit zone – which has a military surveillance station – is restricted. Or you can make the ascent to the eerie old summer villa of the last Italian king *(200m uphill on paths | 30 mins walk). ◫ D8*

ARCHÁNGELOS

(◫ F–G 8–9) **Archángelos (pop. 5,500) is a good example of how tourism does not have to be synonymous with the disappearance of everything that is fundamental to the charm of a place.**

It shares this aspect with Afántou, yet the historic centre of Archángelos is far more appealing. There are old, whitewashed houses and unevenly paved alleyways. The locals always seem to have time to spare. Old traditions still mean something in the "village of the Archangel" – especially on Good Friday and Saturday as well as on Carnival Sunday. The next beach is 3km away, below the town at Stegná.

SIGHTSEEING

CHURCH

Like a bejewelled, snow-white finger, the bell tower of the church of the Archangel Michael dominates the similarly white houses of the old part of Archángelos. The structure, with its delicate air, is a remnant of the Italian occupation. The church itself dates back to the mid-19th century. The most interesting feature is the typically Rhodian mosaic in the inner courtyard made of black and white pebbles. ◷ *10–15 mins*

KNIGHTS' FORTRESS 🐗

On a hill on the edge of the village stand the ruins of a castle built by the Knights of St John, commissioned by Grand Master Orsini in the middle of the 15th century. Close to the entrance, several coats of arms are to be seen carved into the walls, including the Orsini crest and the number 1467, the year the castle was completed. From the castle, you have a fine view over the white silhouette of the historic part of the village. It is well suited to a picnic, and best visited on foot. ⏱ *15–30 mins*

EATING & DRINKING

AFÉNTIKA

This small, unspectacular taverna, in which elderly local residents often get together in the evenings to watch television, serves up a particularly good Greek salad. Made according to the traditional recipe, twigs and leaves from the caper bush, marinated in vinegar, are also added. The proprietor is extremely friendly and often lets you have an ouzo or *soúma* on the house – and consequently has built up quite a following among Archángelos' holiday guests! Dishes that are not actually on the menu can be prepared specially, if ordered in advance. *Daily in summer from 10am | in the centre, behind the Legend Bar on the road to the post office | tel. 22 44 02 37 56 | €*

INSIDER TIP
Deliciously soft thorns

HELLAS

The owner Stélios grew up in Germany, so his restaurant has some German touches, despite its very Greek name. Regular customers particularly appreciate the *tirokftédes* (cheese balls). There may be live music if guests bring their own instruments. *Mon–Sat from 5pm, Sun from 7pm | beside the town hall | tel. 69 74 18 19 59 | €*

SHOPPING

Traditionally, Archángelos is seen as the island's pottery village. There are a number of ceramics workshops on the main road between Rhodes Town and Líndos.

SPORT & ACTIVITIES

JUNGLE TOUR

Although the ✅ jungle tour with Níkos Pápas covers a distance of only 4km, it is packed with unusual experiences. After a cup of coffee, Níkos starts the day off with a dance lesson. Then the actual tour begins, which leads you mostly through a dry riverbed. Here, Níkos explains the flora and geology of the location, turning out to be a great multilingual talker. There are stalls along the way where you can sustain yourself with fresh fruit. At the end, and following a cooking lesson, Níkos serves food on tables in the riverbed. *Tour 28 euros incl. food | tel. 69 38 19 00 41 | nikospapas.nl*

INSIDER TIP
An eccentric experience

AROUND ARCHÁNGELOS

🔟 **STEGNÁ** 🌴
3km from Archángelos / 10 mins by car

Charáki offers sympathetically designed B&Bs below towering castle ruins

This remote beach village can be reached via a winding road. The 300m-long, sandy beach at Stegná is perhaps not as beautiful as the one at Tsambíka, but the bay is greener and the food at the shady tavernas is down-to-earth, good-quality Greek fare. In the seafood taverna *Perigiáli (daily | tel. 22 44 02 34 44 | €€)* on the coastal road you can order *Germaní*: these brown rabbitfish got their name during World War II thanks to their spikes and camouflage colour. *G9*

14 CHARÁKI

9km from Archángelos / 15 mins by car

Fifty years ago, only a handful of summer houses stood on the pebble beach here. Many of them belonged to farmers from the villages of Malónas and Mássari further inland, where people still live from the cultivation of oranges and mandarins. Since then, Charáki has become a popular bathing resort, but without the huge hotel blocks. Visitors stay mostly in small guesthouses and holiday apartments. A pedestrianised beach promenade, with cafés, restaurants and bars, adds to the flair of the village. Take a look at the small *Ágii Apóstoli Chapel* on the village square which was decorated inside in 1997 and 1998 in the traditional style by the monks of the autonomous republic of Mount Athos. *F9*

15 FÉRAKLOS FORTRESS 🐗

9km from Archángelos / 15 mins by car

On a hill just outside Charáki lie the ruins of the fortress of the Knights of St John, Féraklos, which is illuminated in the evening. It is assumed that a castle stood here in the days of antiquity. What is certain is that there was a Byzantine fortress on the site which was captured by the Knights of St John in 1306. In 1470, Grand Master Orsini had it renovated. The fortress was used mostly as a prison for the prisoners of war taken by the Order, and as a place of exile for knights who were guilty of misconduct.

From the north side, there is a beautiful view across the fertile land around Malónas and Mássari and over the bay and sandy beach at the base of the hill. Above the bay, a touching gem is to be found hewn into the rock face: the tiny chapel *Ágia Agáthi* (⏱ 5 mins). It is said to have been constructed in the 12th or 13th century.

Agáthi Bay, which is a 30-minute walk from Charáki, boasts a pretty, sandy beach. Its 200 metres are usually rather quiet except in high summer, and three beach bars have set out their tables in the sand. The fortress is most easily reached from the beach access road, but sturdy shoes are recommended. ⌱ F9

KÁMIROS

(⌱ D2) **Sunbathing and sightseeing – you can get the best of both worlds in ⭐ Kámiros.**

First visit the excavations in the ancient town, followed by the beach and the waterfront tavernas. You can spend a whole day in the town, which is easily reached by bus.

SIGHTSEEING

EXCAVATIONS

Fed up with temples and ancient gods? Here you can find out how normal folk lived over two millennia ago. Kámiros was the smallest of the first three Rhodian cities and had its heyday in the sixth century BCE. The town was built on a slope, and the view from the houses spans green fields, pine woods and olive groves. Inhabitants of the upper part of town could even see the coast. You can still enjoy the same view today because no hotel or industrial plant stands in the way at the moment. The residents, however, paid dearly for their town's exquisitely beautiful location. In 226 BCE, an earthquake destroyed almost every building, but the town was rebuilt. Around three centuries later, in 142 CE, another major quake razed Kámiros to the ground. This time no one wanted to stay, and Kámiros was abandoned.

The ruins of "Rhodian Pompeii" date largely from the third and second centuries BCE. The hillside city was built as a series of terraces. The lower terrace was hewn into the rock, supported by mounds of earth and a retaining wall and enlarged to form the *agorá*, or market place. To each side, there once stood shrines, statues and residential buildings. The small temple in the centre was probably dedicated to Apollo.

To the east of this, there is a festival ground with low tiers of seats for spectators. This was probably the venue for rituals in honour of Apollo, and the start of processions to a hilltop temple to Athena. To the west, the arena borders a residential area that lies directly on the ancient main thoroughfare. This leads past a public baths and a fountain house (in many places, ceramic pipes hark back to the ancient water supply and drainage system) and further residential areas as far as the acropolis. Only a few traces of its once magnificent buildings remain. *May–Oct daily 8am–7.45pm, Nov–April Tue–Sun 8.30am–2.40pm | admission 6 euros | ⏱ 45–70 mins*

EATING & DRINKING

OLD KÁMIROS

Located opposite the side road leading to the excavations and directly in front of the bus stop, the more traditional of the two beach-front tavernas is simply furnished but known for its friendly service.

Langoustines and other shellfish are kept in the large basin – you may be able to haggle over the price. *Daily | tel. 69 45 41 17 30 | €€*

BEACHES

The beach in front of both tavernas is the nicest. Both serve food to customers on the free sun loungers. The beautiful sandy bay makes for a great beach day drenched in history.

AROUND KÁMIROS

16 KÁMIROS SKÁLA

13km from Kámiros / 15 mins by car

A few isolated houses, an occasional

The inhabitants of ancient Kámiros would have enjoyed the same marvellous views

excursion boat and a handful of fishing vessels at the quay in front of the low-lying rocks. The boats sail over from the small islands off the coast of Rhodes, bringing their catches ashore.

Locals gather on the large veranda of the taverna *Altheméni (daily | tel. 22 46 03 13 03 | €–€€)*, to eat fish and succulent pork chops served with Greek salad and marinated capers. With plenty of room between the tables and Greek music playing in the background, the taverna has hardly changed since 1957 when the owner's great-grandfather fed the entire family with the catch from his tiny fishing boat, which still stands prettily decorated on the veranda. *B8*

17 KASTRO KRITÍNIAS 🐗

16km from Kámiros / 25 mins by car
Dating back to the time of the Crusaders, this small castle holds a solitary position overlooking the vast Aegean Sea. The castle is open to the public and is just a five-minute walk from the car park. You can also spend a leisurely hour on the small shady veranda of the welcoming *Kritinia taverna (€)* beneath the car park. *Kritinía | 20–35 mins | B–C8*

18 CHÁLKI

12 nautical miles from Kámiros Skála, 35 nautical miles from Rhodes Town, ferry crossing approx. 35 mins or 75 mins
The tiny island of Chálki is worth the short boat ride. Only 200 people now live there, but the main village of

A Mediterranean dream: the village of Nimborió on the island of Chálki

Nimborió is really picturesque. As you enter the harbour, notice the old houses painted in pastel colours. More and more of them are gradually being renovated and rented out as holiday homes.

The local minibus or the island's taxi will shuttle you to the three beaches, to the deserted village of *Chorió* with its Crusaders' castle, and to the monastery *Ágios Ioánnis* in the island's far west. This region shows how rugged and barren the landscape can be on the Greek Aegean islands.

The fastest way to get to Chálki is to take the *catamaran (12ne.gr)*, which runs several times a week from Rhodes Town, making a day trip possible. In summer, passenger ferries to the island depart from Kámiros Skála several times a day, and several times a week in winter. The large car ferries from Rhodes to Crete also usually dock in Chálki. 📖 *A–B 1–2*

SLEEP WELL IN THE CENTRE

QUIET DAYS BY THE SEA

Stegná looks as though it comes from the pages of a picture-book: the village is fronted by a long, sandy and uncrowded beach where there's plenty of room for everyone to sunbathe in peace, and the tavernas all serve authentic Greek cuisine. There are two buses a day up to Archángelos and a daily boat to Rhodes Town or Líndos. The rooms at the *Delfini Beach Hotel (15 rooms, 6 studios | on the beach | tel. 22 44 02 33 23 | delfinistegna.com | €€)* are stylish, modern and remarkably reasonable. You'll be hard pressed to find a better deal.

INTO THE WOODS & INTO HISTORY

The *Elafos Hotel (22 rooms | Epar. Od. Kalavardas-Empona 71 | Salakos | elafoshotel.gr | tel. 22 41 04 48 08 | €€)* is one of the most unusual hotels on Rhodes. Built in 1929 by and for Italians, it's an architectural oddity in the luxurious style of days gone by. Sure, it's located a long way from the coast, so you'll need a car to reach the beach, but the advantage is a peaceful holiday in a nostalgic and historic setting. There are maps for exploring the area on foot or by bike, and the restaurant *Elafki* is on site.

DISCOVERY TOURS

Want to get under the skin of the island? Then our discovery tours provide the perfect guide – they include advice on which sights to visit, tips on where to stop for that perfect holiday snap, a choice of the best places to eat and drink and suggestions for fun activities.

A must-see destination: the Acropolis of Líndos

DISCOVERY TOURS OVERVIEW

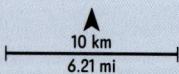

Mandrikó
Akra Katsoúni
Akra Kopriá

Alimiá
Alimiá
Ág. Theodóros
Makri I.
Strongilí
Tragoussa
Nisaki

Kritinía
Embona

Akra Kefálos
Hálki
Horió
Emborió
Akra Mírtos

Lakki
Ág. Isídoros

Akra Armenistís
Siána

Monólithos
Istrios
Profília

Mediterranean
Sea

Órmos
Apolakkiás

Apolakkiá
Arnítha
V.

Mesanagrós

Lahania
Kattavía
Hóhlakas
Ágios
Pavlos
Plimmíri
Akra Vígl

Akra
Prasonísi
Prasonísi

10 km
6.21 mi

Rhodes at a glance

①

The Old Town in depth – a day in the capital

②

Up & down the mountains

①

Cycling through quiet villages

④

Ródos
Ormos Triánta

Ialisós
Kremastí
Sgouroú
Akra Zonári

EO95
Koskinoú
Akra Vódi
Thermes Kallithéas

Soroní
Pastída
Damatría
Maritsá
Kalithiés
Faliráki

Fánes
Epáno Kalamónas
③
Psínthos
③
Akra Ladikoú

alákos
Dimiliá
Afándou
③
①
Eleoússa
Loutáni
Kolímbia

Apóllona
Arhipoli
Akra Vágia

Platánero

EO95

Malónas
Arhángelos

Gaidourás
Másari
Haráki

Láerma

①
Kálathos
Pilónas
Akra Ág. Emilianós

Kontári
EO95
Lárdos
Líndos

Asklipiío
Ormos Lárdos
Péfki
Akra Lárdos

Gennádi

❶ RHODES AT A GLANCE

➤ Once round the whole island
➤ The island's most beautiful monastery with a view towards Asia Minor
➤ Ancient ruins and a surfers' beach
➤ Regional shopping, a castle to climb and authentic taverns for lunch
➤ Stop for a coffee in a village square
➤ Just take a quick look at Líndos, otherwise you'll never leave
➤ Dinner in the island's most authentic village

📍 Rhodes Town

🏁 Rhodes Town

🔄 approx. 240km

🚗 2 days (4½hrs total driving time)

ℹ️ Pick up the keys for your rental car on the evening before if the rental agency does not open before 8am, and return them at 9pm the following day.

---

❶ **Rhodes Town**	
13km 15 mins	
❷ **Filérimos**	
31km 30 mins	
❸ **Kámiros**	
13km 15 mins	
❹ **Kámiros Skála**	
22km 20 mins	
❺ **Siána**	

START EARLY WHEN IT'S STILL COOL

Depart from ❶ **Rhodes Town ➤ p. 38** *in the morning around 8am and head towards the airport. From the centre of Ialissós (Triánda) ➤ p. 55, follow the signs up to* ❷ **Filérimos ➤ p. 55**. The open view of the coast and the island's mountains to the southwest gives you a real feel for the beauty of the Rhodian landscape and offers great photo opportunities.

Head back to the coastal road and follow it until you reach the excavations of the ancient city of ❸ **Kámiros ➤ p. 96**. It's best to arrive in the early morning because the archaeological site doesn't have any shade. A good place to take a break afterwards is the fishing harbour ❹ **Kámiros Skála ➤ p. 97**, an ideal spot to watch the local fishermen at work.

UP INTO THE MOUNTAINS AND TO THE CASTLE

Afterwards, travel up to the large mountain village of ❺ **Siána ➤ p. 76**. It is worth taking a short break to

admire the **church gate** which is often covered in a wealth of blossom. *You can park in the car park below the road directly by the church.* Drive on a bit further and climb up to the **castle ruins** of ❻ **Monólithos ➤ p. 74**, from where you can look out over the sea to the neighbouring island of Chálki. If all of this has made you hungry, Monólithos is a good place to have some lunch.

DRIVE ON FOR COFFEE IN THE SOUTH

Continue along the open and largely untouched beaches where the winds are sometimes quite strong

5km 5 mins

❻ **Monólithos**

32km 40 mins.

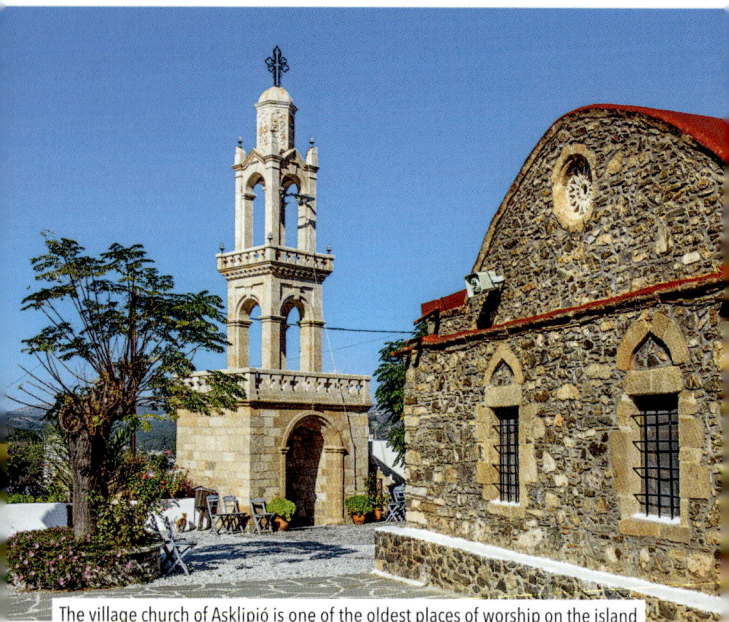

The village church of Asklipió is one of the oldest places of worship on the island

⑦ Kattaviá

9km 15 mins

⑧ Prassoníssi

23km 30 mins

⑨ Lachaniá

18km 15 mins

⑩ Asklipió

9km 10 mins

⑪ Glístra Beach

12km 15 mins

to the southernmost point on the island near ⑦ Kattaviá ➤ p. 78. After a coffee break on the village square, drive along *the well-paved road through the isolated countryside to the island's southern cape* where you will find the surfers' beach ⑧ Prassoníssi ➤ p. 78, which resembles the Sahara in miniature.

First head back to Kattaviá and, from there, continue on towards ⑨ Lachaniá ➤ p. 73. For an authentic culinary experience with a rustic feel, stop in at the taverna **Plátanos**.

SACRED ART AND AEGEAN WAVES

Follow further along the coast towards Kiotári ➤ *p. 70,* *where a small cul-de-sac leads up to* ⑩ Asklipió ➤ p. 71 The frescos on the walls of the **church** in this small mountain village are some of the island's most beautiful. *Almost right next door on the coastal road* ⑪ Glístra Beach ➤ p. 70 , one of the prettiest on the island, will lure you into the water for a swim.

IMMERSE YOURSELF IN PICTURESQUE VIEWS

Shortly before Lárdos ➤ p. 69, turn to the right to head towards Péfki ➤ p. 68 and keep driving through this coastal town to get to ⑫ *Líndos ➤ p. 62.* As you approach this picturesque village from above, you will see its old captains' houses and countless souvenir shops, as well as St Paul's Bay and the broad main beach below. The ancient acropolis lies before you at about eye-level. You'll now realise why it is worth spending another entire day here.

⑫ **Líndos**

51km 55 mins

VISIT A TYPICAL TAVERNA

The road between Líndos and the island's capital makes for an easy and quick drive back to ❶ Rhodes Town where you will arrive around 9pm if you choose to return on the same day. If you do not have to turn in your rental car until the next morning, you should definitely drive on to the large village of Archángelos ➤ p. 93, where you can dine among the locals in one of the country-style tavernas in the centre of town before making your way back to Rhodes Town.

❶ **Rhodes Town**

❷ THE OLD TOWN IN DEPTH – A DAY IN THE CAPITAL

➤ A pavement quest to find the Knights of St John
➤ The most beautiful harbour
➤ Lions, dolphins and nudes – sculpture in the Archaeological Museum
➤ Shop with philosophers on Socrates Street
➤ Discover Jewish, Turkish and Greek culture

📍 Néa Agorá   🏁 Néa Agorá

🔄 approx. 5km   🚶 1 day (1½ hrs total walking time)

ℹ️ Wear flat shoes with non-slip soles!

The fountain on Platía Argirokástrou

TAKE IN THE VIEW

All bus routes from the holiday resorts into town end at the **❶ Néa Agorá** ➤ p. 46. First off, *stroll through the inner courtyard* with its many barbecue stands and a handful of jewellers and souvenir shops and make your way to the two kiosks opposite, which boast the largest selection of international newspapers and magazines on the island. *Pass between the kiosks to come out on the harbour side of the Néa Agorá*, which is home to some tempting pastry shops. If you can resist the delicious cakes and ice cream sundaes on offer, *cross the street* and sit down on one of the many benches to take in the colourful array of excursion boats and sailing yachts before you.

❶ Néa Agorá

700m

❷ Ágios Nikólaos

Then *wander past the restored windmills on the eastern pier to the medieval fortress tower* **❷ Ágios Nikólaos**. This is the best place to take a photo of the Old Town centre across Mandráki Harbour ➤ p. 47. You can also get a good snapshot of the huge cruise ships often docked in the neighbouring Emborikó harbour. That might work well for a selfie.

INSIDER TIP
The big boys

INTERESTING MUSEUMS

600m

❸ Aphrodite Temple

40m

❹ Museum of Modern Greek Art

150m

❺ Museum of Archaeology

Once you are back at the mill pier, *follow the traffic over the short bridge into the Old Town*. Behind the parked cars, it is easy to overlook the remains of an ancient **❸ Aphrodite Temple**. Art lovers should head to the right and explore the **art gallery** of the **❹ Museum of Modern Greek Art** ➤ p. 48. Go a few steps further and you will find yourself on the *Platía Argirokástrou*. Alongside the small pyramids of stone cannonballs, this square is home to a beautiful fountain. *Walk straight on for another 50m* until you reach the **❺ Museum of Archaeology** ➤ p. 42, which housed

108

the large hospital run by the Knights of St John. Even if you are not really into art, you should still definitely take a look. The two-storey arcades of the inner courtyard provide a great photo opportunity, and the large hospital ward of the Order of St John is like no other in the world. A shady garden invites you to have a rest among the greenery.

GIVE YOUR FEET A BREAK AND GAIN AN OVERVIEW

The cobblestoned Avenue of the Knights ➤ *p. 44 climbs gently uphill, past the 600-year-old inns of the*

Socrates Street is the best place to find a souvenir

crusaders to the magnificent ❻ Palace of the Grand Master ➤ p. 44. *After inspecting the palace, it is time to treat your feet to something special. Head right out of the Palace of the Great Master and go left on Odós Orféos.* Give your feet a break in ❼ Magía Fish Spa ➤ p. 53, courtesy of the small fish in the glass tubs who like to nibble away at your toes. After that, head up to the top of the ❽ Clock Tower ➤ p. 45 to get a good overview of the entire town. The entrance fee includes a refreshing drink.

BROWSING AND SHOPPING

The ❾ Mosque of Suleiman ➤ p. 45 with its towering minaret marks the beginning of the most dangerous part of the tour, at least for your bank account. *Head down* ❿ Odós Sokratoús ➤ p. 45, where you can shop at your leisure and then shop some more. Shops selling jewellery, leather goods and souvenirs line Socrates Street on both sides. The best places to stop for a snack are the secluded garden café Socratous Garden ➤ p. 50 at the top end of the street, or Café Kárpathos *(daily)* in the middle, where you can sit under shady trees and watch as people from around the world pass by. If you like quaint places, *head down Odós Sokratoús for another 20m* and check out (on the left) the town's oldest café: Mevlana Shisha Bar ➤ p. 45, orginally known as Kafenío Bekir Karakusu.

INTO THE JEWISH QUARTER

Socrates Street ends at *Platía Ippókratou* with its expensive cafés. If you order a large beer here, you will be presented with a four-pint boot-shaped glass. Go past the many souvenir shops along the street until you come to *Platía Evréon Márytron*, with its noisy parrots, in the former Jewish Quarter of the Old Town. *Odós Dossiádou* is home to the fully restored ⑪ Kahal Shalom Synagogue ➤ p. 46. From here, the route *continues through the narrow and winding streets of the town centre*. The rump of an old ⑫ Windmill on *Odós Pythágora* offers a great vantage point from which to gaze over the rooftops of the Old Town and cast your eyes across the sea towards Asia Minor.

FROM THE PASHAS TO AN UNUSUAL LOST-PROPERTY OFFICE

At the end of Odós Pythágora, in the area around the ⑬ Ibrahim Pasha Mosque *(visitors always welcome except during Friday prayers),* you will find the hippest quarter of the Old Town. It might be a little sleepy in the afternoon, but in the evening, it really comes to life. *Follow Odós Sofokléous to get to the* ⑭ Platía Doriéos ➤ p. 46 where the attractive Rejab Pasha Mosque and two pleasant cafés await. *Continue along to the Byzantine church of* ⑮ Ágios Fanoúrios ➤ p. 46. In a way, this church is the town's lost-property office because, on request, Saint Fanoúrios helps people to find lost and forgotten items. After taking a look inside, head past the *Sultan Mustafa Mosque to what were once the* ⑯ Turkish Baths.

Afterwards, you can take another stroll *through the area around Socrates Street*. Spend the rest of the evening in one of the characteristic and enjoyable Old Town tavernas before returning to ❶ Néa Agorá to catch a bus or taxi back to your hotel.

⑪ **Kahal Shalom Synagogue**

500m

⑫ **Windmill**

250m

⑬ **Ibrahim Pasha Mosque**

250m

⑭ **Platía Doriéos**

200m

⑮ **Ágios Fanoúrios**

150m

⑯ **Turkish Baths**

950m

❶ **Néa Agorá**

③ UP & DOWN THE MOUNTAINS

➤ Find peaceful Rhodes in green woodland and small villages
➤ Visit ostriches and butterflies
➤ Plenty of village tavernas for refreshment
➤ Saints and prophets in mountain forests
➤ Find out who can fit inside a plane tree
➤ Peacocks, a forest taverna and a tunnel to seven springs

📍 Faliráki   🏁 Faliráki

🔄 c. 110km   🚗 1 day (4 hrs total driving time)

ℹ️ Take a torch and a towel for going through the tunnels, and provisions for a picnic.
Please note that many of the butterflies in Petaloúdes can only be seen from June to August.

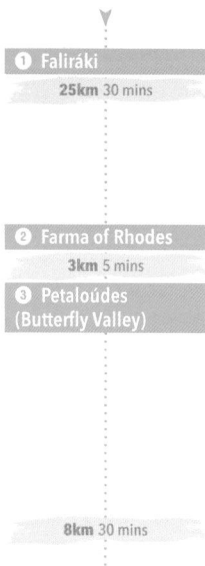

① Faliráki

25km 30 mins

② Farma of Rhodes

3km 5 mins

③ Petaloúdes (Butterfly Valley)

8km 30 mins

OSTRICHES AND BUTTERFLIES

From ① Faliráki ➤ p. 84 , *drive towards the airport. Just past the eastern end of the airport village of Parádissi, signs clearly point the way to a side road that branches off from the main road and leads towards the Butterfly Valley in Petaloúdes.* Especially if you have kids on board, you should take a short detour to see the ostriches and other animals at the ② Farma of Rhodes ➤ p. 89 that lies along the way. Park your car at the lower (first) entrance to ③ Petaloúdes (Butterfly Valley) ➤ p. 88 and *walk upstream and back down again.* If you take a break for a cup of coffee in the taverna at the lower entrance to the valley in August, you will probably find yourself surrounded by colourful fluttering wings.

TIME FOR A LUNCH BREAK

Afterwards, drive on the uphill road past the middle and upper entrances to the Butterfly Valley and the

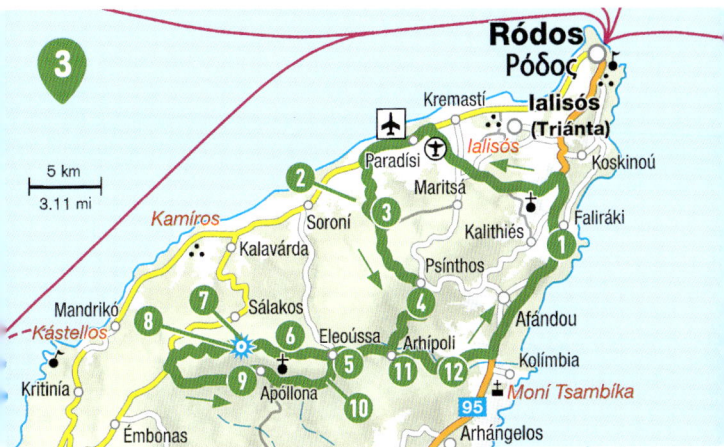

abandoned *Kalópetras* monastery. *As the road contin-ues on, it climbs to the top of a pass and then back down to the large village of* ❹ **Psínthos** ➤ **p. 88**, *where you can eat lunch on the* Platía *or in the* **Artemída House**, *which lies on the road leading to Archípolis.*

When this side road meets the main road from Kolímbia to Eleoússa, turn right and pass through Archípolis and ❺ **Eleoússa**, *with its abundance of water and Italian-style colonial houses, to the isolated Byzantine church of* ❻ **Ágios Nikólaos Fountoúkli** ➤ **p. 92**, *where you can enjoy a picnic.*

CIRCLE THE MOUNTAIN – FOR THE SPORTY

You can enjoy some refreshments at the café of the Alpine-style hotel ❼ **Élafos** ➤ **p. 93** *located in the forest right below the 780m-high* ❽ **Profítis Ilías** ➤ **p. 93**. *Reinvigorated, you can then circle Profítis Ilías on a narrow tarmac forest road (8.5km long); just follow* the signposts to the "Athletic Centre". If the hotel reception agrees, you can also do it on one of the hotel's rental bikes. Whether by car, bike or on foot: you will experience a mostly unknown part of Rhodes!

INSIDER TIP
A short bicycle ride

❹ Psínthos	
13km 15 mins	

❺ Eleoússa	
3km 5 mins	
❻ Ágios Nikólaos Fountoúkli	
6km 10 mins	

❼ Élafos	
1km 30 mins	
❽ Profítis Ilías	
15km 35 mins	

OLD VILLAGES AND AN EVEN OLDER TREE

After you've returned to the Hotel Élafos, drive to the peaceful mountain villages of ❾ **Apóllona** and ❿ **Plataniá**. *You will then find yourself back in Eléoussa before you again pass through* ⓫ **Archípolis** ➤ p. 92. *Just after you leave the village, look to the right* and you will see a hollowed-out 🌳 **tree** below the large pilgrimage church of **Ágios Nektários**, with its decorative frescos. Your children may want to play in the "tree house" and the kiosk nearby sells hot and cold drinks.

INSIDE THE GREEN TUNNEL

Drive through the valley of the Loutáni stream towards the coast, and then follow the signs to turn towards the forest taverna at ⓬ **Eptá Pigés** ➤ p. 92. Ducks and peacocks will come out to greet you before you explore the dark, short tunnel to the spring for a bit of an adventure.

At *Kolímbia, get back on the eastern coastal road* and it is just another 10km back to ❶ **Faliráki**.

In Ágios Nektários Church you won't know what to look at first

④ CYCLING THROUGH QUIET VILLAGES

➤ A tour of rural Rhodes
➤ Stop off in authentic villages
➤ An ancient chapel, alone in a wood
➤ Picnic in a cloister courtyard
➤ Take a break in the village priest's taverna
➤ Swim at Gennádi Beach

📍 Kiotári		🏁 Kiotári	
🕐 55km		🚲 1 day (4½–7 hrs cycling time)	
📶 difficult		↗ 500m	

ℹ Mountain bike and e-bike rental is usually easiest via your hotel; if it's too hot for cycling, consider hiring scooters.
Bike rental: approx. 12 euros/day
Take a picnic!

CYCLING FROM VILLAGE TO VILLAGE

From ① Kiotári ➤ p. 70 where you will start your trip, *follow the coast until you reach the northern edge of* ② Gennádi ➤ p. 72, a village that has retained its truly authentic character. *From here, the road towards Vatí, which is 7km away, forks off from the road circling the island* and leads into the middle of the island along a mostly flat stretch where, if you are lucky, you may spot a stag. *You should definitely cycle into* ③ Vatí *itself* because the village square is well worth a stop.

Continue upwards through the hilly countryside, which was damaged by forest fires but is still full of fruit trees, *to the small church of* ④ Agía Iríni and then pass by ⑤ Taverna Vrisi *(daily | tel. 22 44 06 11 78 | €)* with its simple, good rustic food. *Cycle on through* ⑥ Arnithá with its abundance of flowers, the 19th-century Church of St George and an old drinking fountain.

⑴ **Kiotári**
4km 15 mins
② **Gennádi**
7km 25 mins

③ **Vatí**
8km 30 mins

④ **Agía Iríni**
2km 10 mins
⑤ **Taverna Vrisi**
0.5km 4 mins
⑥ **Arnithá**

A WINDING TRACK WITH GREAT VIEWS

The most difficult stretch of the route lies ahead, but it also offers the best views. *The often dusty field track winds over the 500m-high Koukoúliari hills and after 12km you will come to* ❼ Mesanagrós ➤ p. 77 with its ancient village church and the Village Café ➤ p. 78, which is simple but good for a snack. After a long, incredibly relaxing break among the rather old villagers, head back at around 3pm along the last, mostly downhill stretch.

PICNIC BY THE CHURCH

If you would prefer a picnic, the small pilgrimage church of ❽ Ágios Thomás ➤ p. 78 *in the forest directly below the road to Lachaniá is ideal*, but please be aware that you won't find any drinking water here.

BLESSED ORGANIC VEGETABLES

On the way to ❾ Lachaniá ➤ p. 73 *you will have to manage just one more short ascent.* Right afterwards, you can stop in at Acropole chez Chrissis ➤ p. 73, the coffee house of the village priest, or treat yourself to some of the organic fruit and vegetables. The priest is happy to pose for a photo in his traditional robes.

12km 1½ hrs

❼ **Mesanagrós**

2km 10 mins

❽ **Ágios Thomás**

6km 25 mins

❾ **Lachaniá**

10km 35 mins

No rush! The village square of Lachaniá is ideal for a relaxing stop

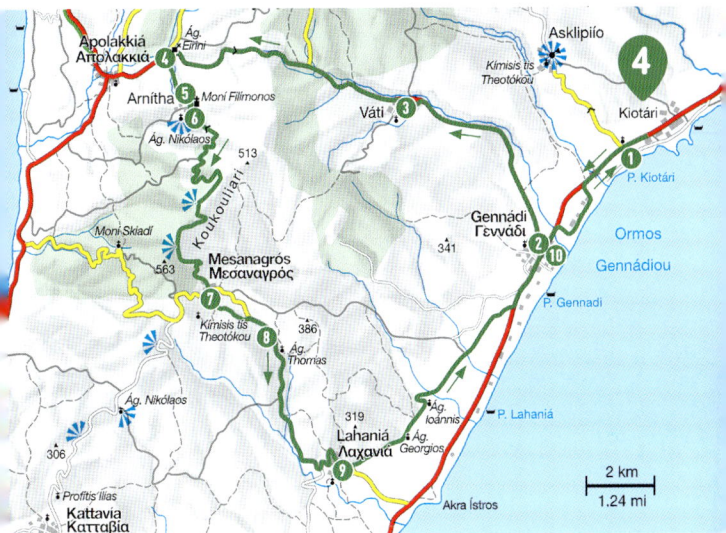

FINALLY YOU CAN JUMP INTO THE SEA

After Lachaniá, a long and straight dirt road forks off from the coastal road and brings you back to ⑩ Gennádi *in 10km. Here you can have a swim before you tackle the last 4km to* ① Kiotári.

⑩ Gennádi		
4km 20 mins		
① Kiotári		

GOOD TO KNOW

HOLIDAY BASICS

ARRIVAL

GETTING THERE

There are direct charter flights from many British airports and most major cities in Western Europe. The flight time from London is around four hours. Passengers on scheduled flights (almost always) have to fly via Athens. Rhodes airport lies 14km to the south of the capital, Rhodes Town. There is a half-hourly bus service into town for 2.60 euros, while taxis cost approx. 30 euros and take around 25 minutes.

+ 2 hours ahead
Greece is two hours ahead of Greenwich Mean Time, seven hours ahead of US Eastern Time and seven hours behind Australian Eastern Time.

GETTING IN

A valid passport is required for entry into Greece (and for trips into Turkey). Children need their own passport.

Adapter Type C
You will need an adapter type C if you want to use a UK plug.

CLIMATE & WHEN TO GO

With the exception of the rainy and stormy months between December and mid-March, any time is a good time to visit. The island's countryside is especially lush and in full bloom between March and May. Less colourful, perhaps, but still with pleasant water temperatures, October or November are also a good choice. July and August are least suitable for hikers and those interested in visiting cultural sites due to the heat.

Bear in mind that many archaeological sites, such as at Kámiros, offer no shade

GETTING AROUND

BUS & FERRY

Buses link almost all the villages around the island with Rhodes Town. The departure point for all buses is at the back of the Néa Agorá market hall. Rhodes Town is served by seven bus lines running between about 7am and 9pm. Up-to-date schedules can be obtained at tourist information offices and *ktelrodu.gr/en*. In the summer months, a Sea Shuttle *(falirakisealines.com)* connects Faliráki and Kolímbia with Rhodes Town and Líndos four times a day from Monday to Saturday.

CAR HIRE

Cars can be hired at the airport, in Rhodes Town and in all holiday resorts.

Drivers only need to hold a valid national driving licence. It is highly recommended to compare prices on the internet. Usually, Greek rental firms hand the hire vehicle over with an almost empty tank. You are expected to return it in the same state and will not get a refund for excess petrol in the tank.

OFFSET YOUR FLIGHT

The return flight is likely to be the most environmentally damaging part of your holiday. A single traveller on a return flight from London to Rhodes generates 926kg of CO_2. You can offset this emission at *myclimate.org* (and other organisations) for around £16. The money is used to fund climate protection projects around the world.

The maximum speed is 50kmh in towns and 100kmh on national roads. Maximum blood alcohol content (BAC) is 0.05%. Right of way is not indicated as such – you will only recognise it by the Stop and Give Way signs on minor roads. At roundabouts, anything coming from the right has right of way, unless signposted otherwise.

In the event of a breakdown, call the rental firm immediately – you are not allowed to arrange repairs yourself.

TAXI

Taxis (dark blue with white roofs) are to be found at the airport, outside the big hotels and at the taxi rank in Rhodes Town *(Mandráki Harbour)*. You can also flag down taxis in the street., or ask your hotel or restaurant to order one for you. Fixed prices are displayed on boards at taxi ranks.

EMERGENCIES

CONSULATES & EMBASSIES
British Embassy (Athens)
1 Ploutarchou | 10675 Athens | tel. 21 07 27 26 00 | ukingreece.fco.gov.uk

Canadian Embassy (Athens)
48 Ethnikis Antistaseos Street | Chalandri | 15231 Athens | tel. 21 07 27 34 00 | international.gc.ca/ country-pays/greece-grece

US Embassy (Athens)
91 Vasilisis Sophias | 10160 Athens | tel. 21 07 21 29 51 | gr.usembassy.gov

EMERGENCY SERVICES
Call 112 – for the police, fire brigade and ambulance.

HEALTH
Well-trained doctors guarantee basic medical care throughout Rhodes. For minor problems, your hotel may be able to recommend doctors or dentists. In more serious cases, you can trust the *Rhodes General Hospital (Odós Christian Barnard 1 | tel. 22 41 36 00 00)* near Ixiá.

Make sure you have travel insurance before you start your trip. Emergency treatment in hospitals is free of charge, and you can be treated for free by doctors if you present the European/Global Health Insurance Card. However, in practice doctors do so reluctantly and it is better to pay cash, get a receipt and then present your bills to the insurance company for a refund.

Most towns and villages have chemists *(farmakíon)* that are well-stocked and can provide advice.

ESSENTIALS

ACCOMMODATION
All coastal towns and some of the villages inland offer accommodation of all sorts. For a real Rhodian experience, stay in Rhodes Old Town or in the village of Líndos. There are no campsites or youth hostels on the island.

BEACHES
Many beaches are only cleaned in front of hotels and where sun loungers

and parasols are for hire. Lifeguards are only found on the most popular beaches and in peak season. Seaweed that has been washed onto the beach at the beginning of the season is often only removed in May or June. Bathing shoes are recommended on many of the beaches (especially in summer when the sand tends to get extremely hot). Nude bathing is prohibited, but is practised and tolerated on many isolated beaches. The only official nudist beach on Rhodes lies at the southern edge of Faliráki.

DRINKING WATER
You can drink the (chlorinated) tap water everywhere. Still mineral water (metallikó neró) is also available in restaurants and cafés and is usually the same price as in the supermarkets.

INFORMATION
Rhodes Tourist Information
Office Platía Rímini | tel. 22 41 04 43 33 | there is a notice board with ferry and bus time schedules in front of the building. Other offices are next to the Museum of Archaeology and (in summer) inside the cruise ship terminal.

Greek National Tourism
Organisation 5th floor East, Great Portland House, 4 Great Portland Street, London, W1W 8QJ | tel. +44 20 7495 9300 | visitgreece.gr

MONEY
The national currency is the euro. It is possible to exchange money at banks and post offices. Opening times: Mon–Thu 8am–2pm, Fri 8am–1.30pm. You can also withdraw cash using your credit card at ATMs.

HOW MUCH DOES IT COST?

Hire car	from 35 euros per day for a small car
Petrol	approx. 2 euros per litre premium
Coffee	1.50–2.50 euros for a cup of mocha
Snack	2.80–4 euros for gyros and pitta bread
Parasol	8–15 euros for a parasol and two sun loungers
Parasailing	30 euros per person

NATIONAL HOLIDAYS
The moveable feasts are scheduled according to the Julian calendar. In many villages, a ✅ festival with music, dancing and drinking is held on the local saint's day. Ask locals for details.

1 Jan	New Year's Day
6 Jan	Epiphany
25 March	Independence Day; Annunciation Day
March / April	Good Friday; Easter
1 May	Labour Day
June	Whitsun
15 Aug	Assumption Day
28 Oct	National Holiday
25 / 26 Dec	Christmas

POST
Post offices are generally open Mon–Fri 7.30am–3pm. The main post office in Rhodes Town (Platía Dimarchíou |

Mandráki) stays open until 8pm. Longer opening hours apply in resorts.

PHONES & MOBILE PHONES

In some areas on the island, Turkish networks are stronger than Greek ones; if you don't want to phone via Turkey, you must search for a different roaming partner manually.

Dialling codes: Greece 0030 followed by the telephone number. To call the UK, dial 0044; Ireland, 00353; the USA, 001; Australia, 0061; then dial the local code without "0" and then the individual number.

SHOPS

In the resorts shops are usually open daily 10am–11pm. In the towns and cities, shops with a predominantly local customer base are open Mon–Sat 10am–1.30pm and Tue, Thu, Fri 5.30–8pm; larger supermarkets open 8am–8pm.

TIPPING

Tips are expected (5–10 per cent), and should be left on the table when leaving.

TOILETS

Many toilet facilities on Rhodes are equipped with the latest Italian sanitary installations. Be aware that in *all* toilets you are not allowed to flush even toilet paper down the drain (use the bin provided); the paper clogs the narrow drains and septic tanks.

WIFI

Almost all hotels, bars, cafés and tavernas offer free WiFi.

WEATHER

High season
Low season

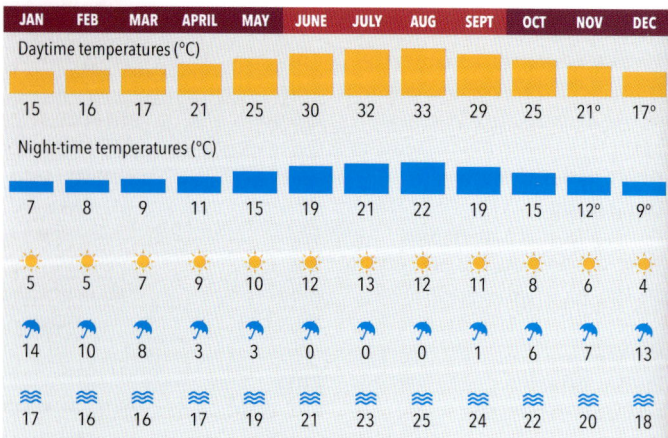

	JAN	FEB	MAR	APRIL	MAY	JUNE	JULY	AUG	SEPT	OCT	NOV	DEC
Daytime temperatures (°C)	15	16	17	21	25	30	32	33	29	25	21°	17°
Night-time temperatures (°C)	7	8	9	11	15	19	21	22	19	15	12°	9°
Hours of sunshine per day	5	5	7	9	10	12	13	12	11	8	6	4
Rainfall days per month	14	10	8	3	3	0	0	0	1	6	7	13
Sea temperature (°C)	17	16	16	17	19	21	23	25	24	22	20	18

☀ Hours of sunshine per day   🐦 Rainfall days per month   ≈ Sea temperature (°C)

USEFUL WORDS & PHRASES

SMALLTALK

Yes/no/maybe	ne/ˈochi/ˈissos	Ναι/ Όχι/Ίσως
Please/Thank you	parakaˈlo/efcharisˈto	Παρακαλώ/ Ευχαριστώ
Good morning/good evening/goodnight!	kalliˈmera/kalliˈspera/ kalliˈnichta!	Καλημέραμ/ Καλησπέρα!/ Καληνύχτα!
Hello/ goodbye (formal)/ goodbye (informal)!	ˈya (su/sass)/ aˈdio/ ya (su/sass)!	Γεία (σου/σας)!/ αντίο!/Γεία (σου/ σας)!
My name is …	me ˈlene …	Με λένεÖ …
What's your name?	poss sass ˈlene?	Πως σας λένε?
Excuse me/sorry	me sigˈchorite/ sigˈnomi	Με συγχωρείτε / Συγνώημ
Pardon?	oˈriste?	Ορίστε?
I (don't) like this	Afˈto (dhen) mu aˈressi	Αυτό (δεν) ουμ αρέσει

EATING & DRINKING

Could you please book a table for tonight for four?	Klisˈte mass parakalˈlo ˈenna traˈpezi ya aˈpopse ya ˈtessera ˈatoma	Κλείστε αςμ παρακαλώ ένα τραπέζι γιά απόψε γιά τέσσερα άτοαμ
The menu, please	tonn kaˈtaloggo parakalˈlo	Τον κατάλογο παρακαλώ
Could I please have … ?	tha ˈithella na ˈecho …?	Θα ήθελα να έχω …?
more/less	pjo/liˈgotäre	ρπιό/λιγότερο
with/without ice/ sparkling	me/choˈris ˈpa–go/ anthrakikˈko	εμ/χωρίς πάγο/ ανθρακικό
(un)safe drinking water	(mi) ˈpossimo näˈro	(μη) Πόσιμο νερό
vegetarian/allergy	chortoˈfagos/allergˈia	Χορτοφάγος/ Αλλεργία
May I have the bill, please?	ˈthelˈlo na pliˈrosso parakalˈlo	Θέλω να πληρώσω παρακαλώ

HOLIDAY VIBES

FOR RELAXATION & CHILLING

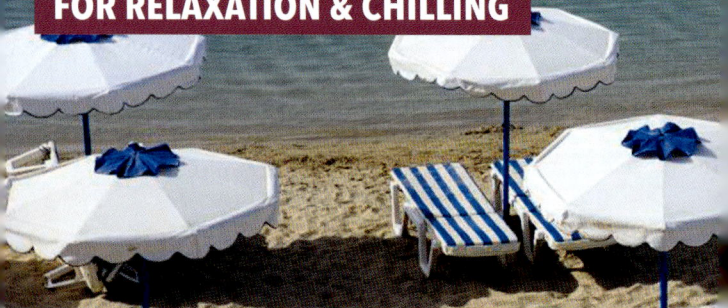

FOR BOOKWORMS & FILM BUFFS

🎥 THE GUNS OF NAVARONE

All-time classic from 1961, still rated as "one of the most exciting films ever made". It won an Oscar for its special effects. And the storyline? David Niven, Gregory Peck and Anthony Quinn fight the German occupiers; Irene Pappas plays the love interest.

📖 REFLECTIONS ON A MARINE VENUS

The quintessential Rhodes novel (1953): Lawrence Durrell paints a vivid picture of the island straight after World War II and before tourism arrived.

📖 RHODES 1306–1522: A STORY

Eureka! A book on the island's history in the age of the knights that is both entertaining and informative. It's narrated and illustrated by well-known caricaturist Vangélis Pavlídis. The book, which was published in 2001, is widely available on Rhodes.

📖 TRIANGLE AT RHODES

In this Agatha Christie short story, her famous Inspector Hercule Poirot investigates a crime on Rhodes. Also available as an audiobook, and a television episode from 1983.

0:58

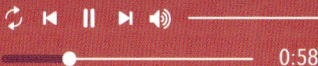

▌ **GIÓRGOS DALÁRAS – KÓKKINO TRIANDÁFILLOU**
One of the best songs by the "Greek Bruce Springsteen".

▶ **MARÍA FANDOÚRI** – STIN ELLÁDA SÍMERA
The well-known singer performs this song by famous composer Míkis Theodorákis.

▶ **ÉLENA PAPARÍZOU** – MY NUMBER ONE
To date this has been Greece's only winning entry at the Eurovision Song Contest.

▶ **NÁNA MOÚSKOURI** – SUMMER HEART
The major star sings a romantic melody about Rhodes.

▶ **FRANKOSYRIANI**
The biggest hit of the underground music Rembetiko – you'll hear it in most of the nightclubs.

Your holiday soundtrack can be found on **Spotify** under **MARCO POLO** Greece

Or scan this code with the Spotify app

ONLINE

RHODESGUIDE.COM
Information on accommodation, events and travel tips. Great photos and videos, too

MYLITTLENOMADS.COM
A section on "Rhodes with kids" provides tips, lists and personal advice specifically for family holidays.

FACEBOOK: LINDOS, RHODES
Líndos visitors swap news and views on various themes to do with Líndos. The notice board also features lots of tips and events.

CRUISETIMETABLES.COM
For anyone wanting to know more about the big cruise liners that come to Rhodes harbour every day and the implications on the numbers of visitors to the Old Town and Líndos.

MARINE TRAFFIC
The sea around the island gets very busy, and this app allows you to get information about the ships in your view and their routes.

INDEX

WE WANT TO HEAR FROM YOU!

Did you have a great holiday? Is there something on your mind? Whatever it is, let us know! Whether you want to praise the guide, alert us to errors or give us a personal tip – MARCO POLO would be pleased to hear from you.

Please contact us by email:

sales@heartwoodpublishing.co.uk

We do everything we can to provide the very latest information for your trip. Nevertheless, despite all of our authors' thorough research, errors can creep in. MARCO POLO does not accept any liability for this.

Credits

Cover picture: Traditional white house in Líndos (Vladimir Zhoga/Shutterstock.COM)
Photos: K. Bötig (127); W. Dieterich (6/7, 97, 118/119); R. Hackenberg (14/15); huber-images: L. Da Ros (34/35, 78/79), D. Erbetta (95), Kaos03 (24/25), M. Ripani (100/101), Schmid (26/27), R. Schmid (12/13, 52); laif: J. Gläscher (10), B. Jaschinski (19); laif/robert harding: N. Farrin (56/57); H. Leue (124/125); Lookphotos: I. Pompe (65); Lookphotos/Avalon.red (80/81, H. Wohner (64); mauritius images (27, S. Beuthan (45), P. Eastland (28), M. Habel (62), W. Layer (114), H.P. Merten (8); mauritius images/Alamy: R. Cracknell (51), I. Dagnall (22/23), D. Delimont (31), P. Forsberg (30/31, 48, 84), Frantic (110), R. Jank (43), N. Korzhov (46/47), L. Kovalic (90), L. Kovalik (9), J. Moravcik (89), C. Moustafellou (92), S. Outram (back flap), O. Panasenko (inner and outer flaps), A. Starikov (58/59), Viliam.M (2/3); mauritius images/Alamy/Aegean Photo (98/99); mauritius images/Alamy/Geogphotos (67); mauritius images/Alamy/Hackenberg-Photo-Cologne (11, 72); mauritius images/imagebroker: R. Franken (70/71, 106, 108), Ch. Handl (68, 116/117); mauritius images/Radius Images (74/75); mauritius images/Westend61: T. Haupt (38/39); mauritius-images/Alamy/parasola.net (76); picture-alliance/akg-images (20); shutterstock: Lubos K (32/33, 86/87); E. Wrba (44)(76); picture-alliance/akg-images (20); E. Wrba (44, 117)

GPSR Compliance: MairDumont GmbH, Marco-Polo-Str, 73760 Ostfildern, Deutschland. Email: info@marcopolo.de

4th Edition – fully revised and updated 2025
Worldwide Distribution: Heartwood Publishing Ltd, Bath, United Kingdom
www.heartwoodpublishing.co.uk

© MAIRDUMONT GmbH & Co. KG, Ostfildern
Authors: Klaus Bötig, Hans E. Latzke
Editor: Franziska Kahl
Picture editor: Barbara Mehrl
Cartography: © KOMPASS-Karten GmbH, A-6020 Innsbruck/MAIRDUMONT, D-73760 Ostfildern (pp. 36–37, 102–103, 105, 109, 113, 117, outer flap, pull-out map); © KOMPASS-Karten GmbH, kompass.de under licence from © OpenStreetMap Contributors, osm.org/copyright (pp. 40–41, 55, 60–61, 63, 82–83).
Cover design and pull-out map design:
Eggers+Diaper, Aachen
Page design: Langenstein Communication GmbH, Ludwigsburg

Heartwood Publishing credits:
Translated from the German by Sophie Blacksell Jones, Susan Jones, Thomas Moser, Jane Riester, Jennifer Walcoff Neuheiser
Editors: Felicity Laughton, Kate Michell, Sophie Blacksell Jones
Prepress: Summerlane Books, Bath
Printed in India

MARCO POLO AUTHOR
KLAUS BÖTIG

A prolific travel-guide author, Klaus has known Rhodes for almost a lifetime, and he met his wife here. What he loves most about them both is their authenticity. Despite huge numbers of visitors to the island, Rhodians have kept their Greek identity. This is because, while the island has always integrated change, it remains deeply rooted in its 3,000-year history.
klaus-boetig.de

DOS & DON'TS

HOW TO AVOID SLIP-UPS & BLUNDERS

DO GO IT ALONE

Tour guides live partly off their commission, and the big tour operators factor them in from the beginning. However, remember you can, if you wish, book your own hire car or make your own way round the island via bus or taxi rather than going on organised excursions. Rhodes is in all respects a safe island, and there is no need to be wary of being independent.

DON'T SHOOT!

Many Rhodians enjoy being photographed, but hate it when tourists behave like hunters who shoot anything that moves! Before you take a picture, be sure to get permission with a smile first.

DON'T DRINK IF YOU DON'T WANT TO

Jewellers and leather salesmen like to treat potential customers to a glass of kir royale, whisky, oúzo or sparkling wine while making their sales pitch. Enjoy a glass if you wish, but remember it's not obligatory.

DO DRESS RESPECTFULLY

At the beach and in the tourist resorts Greeks have got used to the sight of plenty of bare skin. In the villages of the interior and in the Old Town, however, scanty clothing is inappropriate. In churches and monasteries, knees and shoulders must be covered, though it is not necessary for women to wear a headscarf.

DON'T BE SURPRISED AT THE PRICE OF FISH

Fresh fish is absurdly expensive in restaurants and tavernas in Greece. You should always ask the price per kilo and watch the fish being weighed in order to avoid unpleasant surprises when you get the bill.